© Copyright 2002 Suzanna Stinnett. All rights reserved.

No part of this publication may be reproduced, stored in a retrieval system, or transmitted, in any form or by any means, electronic, mechanical, photocopying, recording, or otherwise, without the written prior permission of the author.

Printed in Victoria, Canada

```
National Library of Canada Cataloguing in Publication

Stinnett, Suzanna, 1955-
 Open here, you hold the keys / Suzanna Stinnett.
ISBN 1-55395-326-6
 1. Self-actualization (Psychology)  I. Title.
BF637.S4S74 2002         158.1          C2002-905853-8
```

TRAFFORD

This book was published *on-demand* in cooperation with Trafford Publishing.
On-demand publishing is a unique process and service of making a book available for retail sale to the public taking advantage of on-demand manufacturing and Internet marketing.
On-demand publishing includes promotions, retail sales, manufacturing, order fulfilment, accounting and collecting royalties on behalf of the author.

2404 Government St., Victoria, B.C. V8T 4L7, CANADA
Phone   250-383-6864   Toll-free   1-888-232-4444 (Canada & US)
Fax   250-383-6804   E-mail   sales@trafford.com
Web site   www.trafford.com   TRAFFORD PUBLISHING IS A DIVISION OF TRAFFORD HOLDINGS LTD.
Trafford Catalogue #02-1041   www.trafford.com/robots/02-1041.html

*dedicated with love to my mother,
Deanie Stinnett,
muted by Alzheimer's at age 72.
Mother, I carry the memories for you.*

Acknowledgements

The book was edited by Carol Givner. Carol, I am grateful for your enthusiasm and professional support at a critical juncture.

A standing ovation to all women, men and children who are acting on behalf of their visions. You are my inspiration. Keep it up.

To my main support: My husband, J. Patrick Evans, has endured all of this, and still magically holds our love. My sister, Kathy Stinnett, has trusted me, supported me unconditionally, and listened to me my whole life.

Others who have shored me up and kept me going, either through their enduring belief in me, ready friendship, wise counsel, commitment to my health and healing, or their faithful editing: Abba Anderson, Freddie Evans, Deborah Balmino-Graham, Nancy Rocks, Lois Johnson, Molly Albracht, Shanee Mae, Susan Gross, Selena Polston, Karen Stevens, Audrey Stewart, Michelle Straub, Saul Eisen, and Tamara Slayton. This is not a complete list.

And finally, to everyone at the Willow Wood Market, including Larry, who share community with me, bring me consistently excellent espresso, and give me the safe harbor a cafe writer requires.

Preface

The look and the fonts of this book were chosen with regard to ease of reading. My readership consists mostly of women past the age of forty, which means we are coming to terms with the normal vision changes that occur around this time of life. Frankly I believe we have enough challenges without having to strain our eyes when we read. I expect to hear from you about your experience in all aspects of this book.

The art pieces, called visual vacations, are parts of an ongoing series. I work with a combination of low technology and manual forms of glyphic representation in an exploration of my own curiosity about visual languages. These were produced by typing on an Olympia manual typer, going to the copy shop and enlarging the letters until they became organic-looking, then cutting and pasting them into patterns.

I wholeheartedly encourage you to give me feedback. Share this book, talk about it, work with it, and send me all your comments.

I will incorporate your suggestions and requests into the revised edition of this book.

This form of book publishing enables greater communication between writers and readers. It also means that you may find glitches in the visual experience of this book. The world of publishing is in a major transformation of its own, along with all forms of written communication. The book you have in your hand represents one phase of this change. It is a cultural invention made possible by technology, vision and the human capacity for trial and error. How it affects you is all that counts, so please let me know. And thank you for your tolerance of any inconsistencies you may find in the current incarnation of <u>Open Here</u>.

Please come visit me at my website, www.crowsmoons.com. Participate in the cultural process I am striving to stimulate.

Blessings,
Suzanna Stinnett

CONTENTS

Preface   ix

Imagine   xv

Introduction   1
...let your unlimited essence inform
the parameters of your reality

visual vacation #1, Door5   13

Chapter 1: Little Shifts   15
...of attitude...of action...of joy

visual vacation #2, One   32

Chapter 2: Radical Acts   33
...stopping...silence...breathing...noise...
exercise...imaginative play...using intuition...
meditation...writing...optimism...connecting...
asking...candlepower...joy...remediation

visual vacation #3, Welcome Grid   58

Chapter 3: You Are Here   **59**
...our complicated lives...316 choices...
impact...planetary price...guiltless chocolate...
possible futures

visual vacation #4, eieio   **74**

Chapter 4: Clear Your Frontier   **75**
...creative's gremlins...Clutter: Take It Seriously
...little shifts

visual vacation #5: Order   **86**

Chapter 5: The Landing Pad   **87**
...imagination's home base...what works for
you?...portable landing pad

visual vacation #6: Connecting Cells   **94**

Chapter 6: Tending A Wild Garden   **95**
...nourish your brain...foods...supplements...
playtime...future elders

Chapter 7: Imagine It Here   **107**
...visualizing...navigating...imagine faith...see
your guide...portable altar...nature's mystery

visual vacation #8: Riding Herd   **134**

Chapter 8: Writing Through the Window   **135**
...finding the time...reasons for sobs...
the force of your voice

Memory Trigger   **146**

Chapter 9: The Memory Project   **147**
...global anthology...our stories...writing
with community...publish your work

visual vacation #9: Group 9   **154**

Chapter 10: The Great Adventure   **155**
...scoop up the world...tokens of agreement...
earth charter...business...sustainability party

visual vacation #10: Palms   **180**

Chapter 11: Touching Eden   **181**
...imagination and outcomes...historical
precedent...where we might go

visual vacation #11: Illumines   **189**

I Double Dare You   **191**

Reference Section:
Resources, Websites, Books   **193**

Imagine:

You are being carried with urgent speed, perhaps on the back of a fast horse, across the expanse. You have fully discovered your essence and your message, your piece of the sky mandala. Your reason for being has appeared from behind the veil, and you know, with biting certainty, it is critical to the evolution of us all. It is your truth. Your creation. Nothing in all the world, through all of time, could be as crucial as this expression of your love. All of life is waiting for your arrival.

The mandala is not inconceivably huge, just about as big as the sky you see every day. On the other side, and over there, and over there, just out of your sight, others are winging their way. They, too, are carrying their essential message, their personal expression, to join the intricate, exquisite pattern of vibration as we spin together, joyful, into our common destiny.

INTRODUCTION

Rapid fundamental changes are transforming our world.
Your vision is part of that change.

Discovering your unique vision depends upon your ability to imagine a world you would live in tomorrow. By opening a little door of communication, you can begin right now to engage your deep imaginative process. This book is about joyfully opening those doors.

Perhaps you are entering your fifties, a time of great creativity and expansiveness. Or, you may be a young woman starting out in the world with equal portions of uncertainty, excitement and potential. You could be one of the lucky ones -- retired and ready to travel, play, and experience the world in new ways. No matter where you walk in the world today, the unique way you experience and interpret life is critical to the creation of a healthy future.

You may not know what your vision is right now. Don't worry! Finding your vision and your unique form of expression is a playful process made up of tiny deliberate choices.

Each choice has an effect on the quality of your life today and the future of our culture and our world. As you read, you are already beginning to engage your imagination in the process of choosing a path to joy.

I believe imagination is our premium resource. We carry within us the lost diversity this planet needs. Engaging our individual expression, using imagination to inform, expand, and guide us, we can begin to return to Eden.

Early choices may have derailed your inborn connection to an imaginative life. It certainly happened to me. Seeing my early interest in language, my mother taught me to read and write before I started school.

At the age of five, I announced to my parents that I was keeping a pencil and paper by my bed in case I needed to write something down. They looked at each other, smiled supremely, and said, "No you don't." Amazed at their response, I went to bed with a grim sense of determination. *Yes, I do!! And I'll keep writing, but I won't tell anyone about it.*

Creative writing was my earliest calling, and my most natural connection to my imagination. But it took decades for me to find a way to carry it back into the world.

Most of us have had a similar childhood experience. In this culture, it goes with the territory. Our wholehearted, wildly creative, imaginative play was tempered, and often crushed by the limiting beliefs of parents, siblings, educators or other authority figures.

Now, later in life, many of us share the struggle to unmuffle our voices. This conflict manifests as depression, anxiety, or a lost feeling.

Sometimes it's called a mid-life crisis.

The world seems so disinterested in the offerings of the creative mind. Women especially have been ignored in the arts. What we are left with is a background "whine," a little voice that wants us to take the day off.

My own response was to exile myself from a culture that seemed closed to my offerings -- and keep writing. I retreated into my imagination and my observations, watching the world from the unique perspective of the outsider.

As I watched and wrote, I became gripped with the belief that we have enormous unrealized ability to imagine, envision, and create our lives. I see diversity, nature's premium resource, in all of us. Unique perspectives and abilities are woven through us.

As the future becomes now, I see a terrific need for every facet of this originality. And I believe we can now build a bridge into a radiant future -- *a new paradise.*

We must begin now, with small steps, *today*, to recognize and become all that we are meant to be:

Powerfully imaginative, multidimensional beings walking on earth with compassion, joy, and an open-armed inspiration to share with the world.

Here we are now, the material of a metamorphosis. We are love, and we are whole beings. Two things are missing: One is recognition of our resourcefulness. The other is deliberate choice.

With this book I bang the drum to announce the arrival of a culture of imagination. My vision tells me that our transforming culture now needs

all beings in their highest creative state,

interacting, suffusing each others' lives with inner wisdom developed over centuries. We must share our stories, singing them, dancing them, painting, writing and publishing them.

Growing our diversity into a harmonic kaleidoscope of expression, our dreams can then coalesce into a cultural vision.

We are in the beginnings of a renaissance.

We live in a time of tremendous potential for positive change. A sense of urgency rides my wrist, pushing the pen across the paper. I feel we need to shove our arms into the clay elbow-deep, and find the form inside.

How I Came to Write This Book

Facing the gauntlet of breast cancer, I entered the dark realm of treatment determined to bring something back. In the moment of diagnosis, a wall of open doors appeared.

I knew I was being invited into a place few would venture. Perhaps as a way of coping with the sheer terror of what was about to happen to me, I stared into the doors, seeing an opportunity to pull something powerful and unique from this unwelcome experience. Anticipation mingled with dread and grief.

I took these tough emotions, threw them into the fire, and forged roller skates out of them.

My attitude was this: If I was going to go through all this crap anyway, I was damn sure going to get something of value out of it. I was going through those doors.

I had a long time to think about this. I called those two years of cancer treatment my "Davenport Days." I lived on the couch, but I wasn't lounging. I couldn't. I did what chroniclers do: I took notes. I observed, writing, conferring with the flowers of my soul, day in and day out. I sat silent, in a deep place that many people never have a chance to touch. I ventured into my inner limits -- the frontier of my soul.

Killing cancer is a repetitive death. Every round of chemo put me in a dark cave. I stayed there for a few hours or a few days. Each time I emerged again into the light, dripping with gratitude.

Deep in treatment, sleeping has an extra dimension. In one uneasy dream I faced a huge dog with silver fur. It had a very long and unfriendly face. It came out from behind a shrub and blocked my way, waiting for a chance to devour me. I woke in a sweat, and understood this as an inner warning: Become all that you are. *Now*. My writing took on depth. I began to write more truthfully.

At the same time, my doctor urged me to write. Doctor's orders: Write and Rest. She knew the writing would feed me.

When I finally left the cave, I gasped at the brilliant cacophony all around me. I realized with a huge, happy sigh that I am *alive* -- and smack dab in the middle of a renaissance!

A friend asked me why I limited this book, as she said, by directing it to women. I didn't have a quick answer for her. I had to give it some thought. Then it dawned on me. The answer is balance.

A healthy future culture depends upon imaginative flexibility and expression. At the moment I am writing this, however, men's stories, expression and history are still dominant in the literature, decision-making and money-making. So I address this book to women.

Participate now, all of you. After women's stories and creative expression have expanded to match the cultural value and the sheer quantity of men's, we can begin to use everyone's input, moving forward with purpose and a shared vision. Men will benefit from the message of this book as much as women, simply because the whole world needs the inspired imagination and creative leadership of women, now.

Women all over are strengthening their minds and bodies, honing their tools, the zing of sharpening is in the air. I found myself walking in this new world, so new it has not yet recognized itself.

Still, many remain enmeshed in the fear of change. As our culture stumbles and fails, we tiptoe through our days. We sense the crumbling, and try to avoid the broken glass.

Women all around me also reflect the breaking point we've reached. In this chaotic time, fear has an easy grasp on us. Fear of the unknown is a natural part of survival.

During my long inner journey, I was able to stop the vibration of fear long enough to take a good look. Here's the good news: The changes we fear are already here -- and they are fat orange persimmons, sweet with potential. Let us reap this harvest.

The failures of the last decades have given us raw material to create what we want for our future. It is time to sweep up the front steps, reclaim and rename our creative lives.

Our future is limited only by our vision.

In this book I share my discoveries about vision, its close connection to imagination, and the impact of our small daily choices on our creativity. Use this book in a way that works for you -- as a workbook, a guide, or inspiration.

An important point I will make along the way is that whatever works for you *works*. This is testament to our uniqueness. It is time to honor our diversity: Expand it, Enhance it, Use it!

In chapters to follow we will explore how your natural creativity and imagination will help create the positive changes we all desire for our future.

Reading along, you may notice how closely our desires are matched. I intend to show you how profoundly your feminine originality is needed, and how close you already are to that place in your life, where the deep, creative YOU comes pouring forth into your everyday existence.

The rhetoric of modern psychology would have us believe that humans can't really change their behavior -- not much. This may have been true in the past. But notice how radically everything is changing. When the context around us changes, how can we still be the same? Of course we can't. Never have we lived in a time of such rapid change.

Standards that made sense even 25 years ago are no longer useful. We live in a transient, expansive world, and it lives in us.

We cannot afford limiting beliefs. We *are* changing, and we can choose changes that further our dreams and desires. What we are actually choosing is a facility of movement: To move gracefully, deliberately, through the world's mandala, weaving our dreams and desires, adding our all-important uniqueness to the vision. We are making an original imprint and feeling the relief and satisfaction that comes with voicing our essence.

Our planet's diversity lives within us.

Our planet is suffering from a profound loss of diversity. Yet that diversity lives within us! Our own creative energy, our originality and innovation can return a new form of diversity to our natural world.

Do you think you don't make a difference? Lay that one down, honey. You *are* the difference. With every single choice, every day, all day long.

Powerlessness is a cop-out. For example: Do you spend money? Then you are a consumer, and the consumer is all-powerful.

What does the corporate machine run on? CONSUMPTION: Yours and mine.

In this sense, our world is formed on a daily basis by the choices we make. Our future is created in this way. I'm not suggesting a screeching halt to spending, bringing the world economy to its knees. (Not at the moment.) What I am saying is that you have *choice*.

If you have a dollar to spend, you create tomorrow, for better or worse, for yourself and others. If you are in a position to influence others' spending, even in a small way, that power is amplified. This book highlights the path of choices that connect you to your imagination -- and to a brighter future full of interesting possibilities.

Now hold on! This is not about adding more complexity to your overbooked days. I'm going to give you tools to understand and to employ these ideas.

You see, I've realized how little we have to do, in order to start things turning. Start things *turning*. In that moment, all is altered, forever.

> Little things make
> all the big things happen.

HAVE FAITH

Faith is what you choose it to be. For me, there is one thing I have faith in above all else: the imagination. Mine and yours. Every single thing in the world was first imagined, then brought into being. I have absolute faith in our desire and our ability to imagine a paradise on earth. That absolute faith in *you* is how this book got written.

Sister friends, all of this is easier than it looks. Small steps are always within your reach. We will explore joy and playing, inviting your heart and song, seducing your imagination!

Working through this book, you will discover how your positive choices are intricately connected.

Each small act increases the energy for deliberate creative change.

> Let your unlimited essence
> inform the parameters of your reality.

I want to change a lot of things about this world. My optimism and faith have grown through practice, working with the concepts I describe in this book.

As I take little bitty teeny steps, I am growing closer to my vision. I am allowing change to lay opportunity on my plate. I invite it, joyfully. And then I choose what that means for my life.

I want to live on this giant mandala that is the human creative effort, together, with you, with your expression, your input, your imagination, your joy. I want to show you how to choose this expressive, imaginative life.

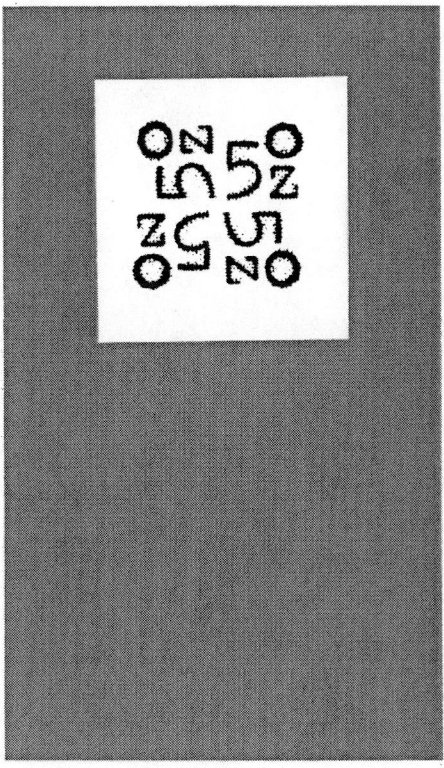

CHAPTER ONE

LITTLE SHIFTS

If you are like many other women today, you have reached a point in your life where the things that matter are changing. You've gotten hints of the cultural veil starting to fray, and you know you have a part in what comes next. The urgency we feel often manifests in a desire to make a difference -- or simply DO something "different" -- to change things.

Little Shifts -- incremental changes -- are comforting, accessible, and amazingly effective. They are life-changing tools.

Expect this turning to your vision to begin to make things easier. Your life exactly as it is now has many elements of what you can be. You may not see them, but your dreams are in your everyday life. Have faith in what you have already created, and allow for the opening and unfolding of your deepest essence, starting right where you are.

Have you ever worked a jigsaw puzzle? Imagine the feeling of fitting in that very last piece. Did you fight with your brother or sister over that piece? It's the glory, right? Now, think about starting a puzzle. Turning over all the pieces, sorting through the color, a mixture of pleasure and dread at the task. But you know you can put this puzzle together. That's not the question.

It will take time, and it will start with one piece fitting another. Perhaps you start puzzles by finding the edges. There's your intelligence at work -- process of elimination. You can see those edge pieces, you can find them, there's a limited number of them, and you can quickly make gains, visually defining the puzzle parameters.

Little shifts are pieces of your life's puzzle,

forming themselves into patterns and areas of color. They make sense as you work with them, one piece at a time.

We *can* make changes, even in our behavior! Make one little shift after another, and suddenly the scattered pieces of your life form a picture.

What causes the big setbacks is expecting the puzzle to be finished before we've really even taken the time to look at it. We decide what we want, and we try to leap into it complete. When that doesn't work, we get discouraged, apply our failure to our self-esteem, and take our expectations down a notch.

There is a better way.

Little Shifts of Attitude

I'm sitting in my favorite cafe, waiting for the caffeine to kick in so I can start writing feverishly in my journal. The waitress sidles up with a coffee refill. She's new. I look up at her face to see sparkly red bindi jewelry glued to her forehead between fawn-colored eyebrows.

Three inches of her muscular mid-section appear just below eye level, which is why I know so much about her navel piercing and lotus tattoo, though I don't yet know her name. I'm mildly intimidated by her youth. I get the feeling she's impatient with me. I begin to muse. *Hm, she probably doesn't want to be here, maybe she resents my freedom, sauntering in at 10:30 in the morning, asking for my latte. Where do I get off?* I refuse the refill, thank you, and she glides away. *Bye-bye, lotus person.*

I stare at the air space that remains. *Great. She hates me.* I glance at my journal page where

I've written in hot pink felt-tip: "Breathe. Smile. Relax." I do this.

Looking up in mid smile, I catch her eye. She flashes a wide grin, a perfect row of white teeth. Her eyes twinkle. *She loves me!* Relief floods my brain. I've just handled a little shift in my attitude. My environment -- including the people in it -- has already responded, and I find the flow moving through me, transforming my world. Attitude shifts can be the most powerful changes we make in our lives.

Here's a little secret. If you can't quite get a grip on your attitude, you can trick it with a little action. Try smiling and making eye contact at the same time. It's an interesting effect, done deliberately. If you're alone, do it in the mirror.

Little Shifts of Belief

When I smiled, and the waitress melted me with her return grin, another shift presented itself -- my belief about what my day might offer.

This takes a little practice, to notice shifts as they show up, and grab onto them. But not as much as you might think! Once you start, you'll keep noticing more, and soon a pattern, a joyful, energetic pattern will emerge. We need lots of reminders as we begin to make changes. I write on index cards, recycled paper, envelopes and paper sacks with bright felt-tip pens. I can prop them up on my desk, type them, or carry them with me. I call these little signs "Trigger Cards."

Forgetfulness is the mortal enemy of deliberately chosen change. Imagination, on the other hand, loves the effective simplicity of a sign pointing the way. Trigger cards easily handle this pesky problem.

Establish a spot somewhere in your morning routine that you know you will see every day. Mirrors are a great place for your notes to yourself. You can use the little suction cup hangers to secure your triggers. Another wonderfully effective place to use trigger cards is in your car. All sorts of little memorized brain paths are set in place -- triggered -- by the very repetitive actions of driving one's car. Trigger cards help set you back on the path to your real destination.

This morning is a good example. I was driving my twenty-year-old Toyota up to our barn. The route takes me through ten minutes of winding country roads with varied green vistas curving off to the right and left along the way. I thoroughly enjoy this drive. However, this morning I'm grumpy. I didn't sleep well, and I haven't had coffee. My car is reliable but eccentric. As I pull away from a light, the engine stutters. This triggers me to start worrying, again, about my choices. Should I have forked out the money for a newer car? Will there be a problem on my drive to the city later? My heart speeds up. I speed up, on the straight stretch along the cemetery. I glance over at the rows of plastic flowers on small graves and think about my mother. She is in the late stages of Alzheimer's, a very sad time in a woman's life.

Note that when I left this morning, I was grumpy, but now I'm depressed and worried. Driving a car is a little bit like watching a movie. A constant stream of visual images trigger floods of emotion. I take a left at the stop sign and start down another beautiful stretch of country road. I take a deep breath and dig around in my pack on the seat next to me, feeling for my little box that holds my trigger cards. I've made these up specifically for my mental and physical habits. Almost any of them will change my frame of mind at any given time. I pull one out and glance at it as I slow for some tight curves. It says, "You're Amazing. BREATHE!! Everything Is OKAY." I place it on the dash in front of me, breathe again, and feel my face relax. When I get to the barn, I make a note to myself. "Make trigger cards for driving." Those of us who have to drive a lot find ways to make it more bearable. We listen to music and to tapes. Trigger cards work the same way, gently redirecting us back to our true intention.

Triggers don't have to be cards, either. I have used discarded ribbon from a birthday present, small toys, anything that reminds me of my inner process.

Experiment with little shifts. If you tend to be grumpy in the morning, write "Hello, Sunshine!" on your note. Or, "Did you take your vitamins?" Focus on the personal connections that you have found helpful in the past. "Time for tea!!" "Congratulations! You made it out of bed!" Write out the key words from a favorite affirmation or a meaningful quote. Everyone has different needs for the kind of language that helps them. One of my best friends is comforted by the phrase "This too shall pass." For me, it's irritating. On the other hand, she was never uplifted by my singing "Bali Hai," while I found it ecstatic. You'll know what works for you. Keep listening. I have a little plastic envelope where I can insert an image or photograph, and keep it on the bathroom mirror so I see it early in the morning. Find something that makes you smile and relax! Pay attention to any phrases or signals that cause irritation or annoyance. Whether it's one of my suggestions or something else in your environment, it may be your imagination telling you "I can do better than that!" Or, "Let me!" Or more precisely, "This will work best for me." Practice listening and responding to this information.

Choosing these little changes, we invite opportunity. We're tugging on the hem of the abundant universe, and it joyfully responds.

Little Shifts of Action

Remember, you are choosing change. You are teaching yourself how to get comfortable with change. You are using the dynamic potential of change to peel away the layers and discover yourself.

One morning on the drive to work, I noticed that I was having a little moment of panic as I entered a big intersection. Not the blinding, gasping kind of panic, just a rumble in my stomach. I realized this was happening every day. It made my brow furrow, which sent the signal to my inner brain to start worrying. (You know, worrying about just anything I could come up with.) This continued the rest of the way to work, and by the time I got there I was wound up, frustrated, distracted, and already tired. I needed my morning break before I even made it to my desk.

So I decided to try something. A small change, a shift of action. The next day, I turned left at that intersection. I took a different route into downtown. This presented a whole flock of changes. The traffic pattern was different. The flow of the streets felt better. I saw people and houses and cars and empty fields I hadn't noticed before. I was five minutes late for work. On the way home, I discovered another piece of the route that took me back into my neighborhood.

The next day, I left early and drove the entire new route. What I found was a much less crowded roadway that took me across a lagoon. Egrets, herons and kingfishers played over the water. On a hillside, two gray appaloosas with long blond manes munched grass near a teepee. I turned on the music and sang along. My mind took a different trip, too. Stimulated by different visuals, sounds, and rhythms, I was triggering different thoughts. I forgot all about the worrisome intersection. My drive to work was filled with new images.

I arrived at work sane and grounded and in a good mood. It meant leaving home about seven minutes earlier, but it changed my whole day.

What was really so different about what I did? Why did it make such a shift in my attitude? I believe it simply made room for my imagination's need for variety and connection.

That little panic I felt might instead have been an oppressive boredom or a growing annoyance. Pay attention to any similar feelings you may have. You don't need to change much to give your imagination the growing room it requires.

Maybe changing your commute route is not an option. That's not really the point. I have found that breaking from the routine in any number of small ways pulls the brain out of that tired rut. The little shift of action stops the old chain reaction. There are other benefits, too. With each shift you create new pathways in your brain. You open up doors you hadn't dreamed possible. In a later chapter, we will look at more ways to keep your brain buzzing at its optimum.

Your shift of action might be putting a note on the bathroom mirror to remind you to say "I love you" to your family. Or to yourself!

It takes time to understand how profoundly these acts enter your life. You are tapping a well inside where your essence begins to flow. You are doing this by choosing change.

We have two choices in life: growth or atrophy. Nothing remains static. Life changes happen with or without your participation.

Choose change at a level you can tolerate.

After one adjustment, you can make another, and another, until you find yourself beginning to tune into the life you desire.

Trying to exclude little shifts from any process of change creates what I call the Boomerang Condition. You bend your will hard over, like making a "U" out of a metal ruler. It will bend, but as soon as you take the pressure off, it comes twanging back at you. Now you can start over, holding your sore nose. Have you ever tried to institute any real change in your life that was not externally imposed? That slump that happens in a week or so is also a kind of boomerang effect. Little shifts make change -- well, *digestible.*

Small adjustments allow for vision, ease, and maneuverability. They also allow for mistakes. Nature evolves imperceptibly, yet with an efficiency and direction we barely comprehend.

Change is incremental.

Changes of Joy

Little shifts steer us back to our hearts. There is a vibrant, almost exotic pleasure in finding our own direction, putting our hearts in place over our culture-driven lives.

A small adjustment breaks the magnetic pull, and relief floods to fill the new space. With relief comes the energy of validation, winging us to the next change. Once we start the turn inward to our deep desire, we feel the pull from within. The momentum has begun.

Smiling is a powerful little shift. While forcing a smile might feel a bit hideous, you can generate it from a deeper place, starting the shift inside. Take a breath. Relax, and see if you can allow the energy of a true smile to surface. Try smiling at yourself in the mirror. This is a small act with profound consequences. Can you do it? What does it feel like? Was it easy? Breathe. Smile. Relax! Recent research has indicated that the brain stimulus that instigates a smile (usually happiness, but not always), also works in reverse. Pull up the corners of your mouth (and hold it for a few minutes, I'm told) and your brain receives the signal cycling back, informing it that you are happy! When I tried this, I ended up laughing hysterically for a while at the ridiculous ease of it all. I decided it was effective enough to offer to my readers.

Smile as you pass a familiar neighbor whose name you do not know. The potential for community just grew. Our lives offer endless possibilities for change every day.

There is a pleasant comfort in little shifts. You can abandon the change and return to it later, pick it up and try it again.

With little shifts, you load the scale slowly back to the life you envision. Not sure what you want for your life? Tiny, accessible changes open the channels of information to yourself. Steadily, light returns.

Believe it or not, incremental changes toward a deliberately imaginative life will open up time.

This is the magic of change. Within the process of change, no matter how small, lies the realm of possibility.

The Practice of Choosing - A Beginning Point

I think most of us would say we want greater ease in our lives. Things have gotten complicated, haven't they? It seems time has been taken away from us. We don't even have time to look at where the time is going.

Tiny changes are right in front of you. They don't take an orchestration, a semester of focused study, to uncover. You can start practicing these shifts today. Look around at your environment with an eye toward change.

Just for fun, and to get a little practice at self-directed change, go hang out in your junk room, garage, or wherever the no-longer-useful ends up.

Breathe, smile, and observe in silence for a moment. See something you'd like to change?

I have a secondary storage area. This is unfortunate, because months can go by without my ever seeing it. But here and there, because it's more convenient than the barn, where things are supposed to be stored, I go and toss something into this space. Naturally, over time, a lot of "tossage" has accumulated.

When I realize there is something in that shed that I need, I am faced with dust, cobwebs, and piles of empty boxes. I'd like to change this. Once a week I spend 15 minutes in that area, dragging out boxes or going through a bag of books I stuck there for some unknown reason. Just 15 minutes. That's a little shift. And that time I spend comes back to me in the form of energy, renewed self confidence, and a sense of well being.

Try a little shift in some troubled area of your home as evidence of directed change. Your practice has already begun.

Teeny Tiny Changes

Understanding little shifts requires a new perspective. Somewhere along the line, we've learned a lie: that we as individuals can't make a difference. Well, that's just *hooey*. Physics reveals that *any* increment of change is *real* change. When you change anything, you change the context in which everything else exists. So try this on: Whatever you change, no matter how tiny, you change it all. Making your life better improves all of life.

This is not a burden to carry, thinking that you must act carefully, that you will upset the balance, hurt others, break something. This is a celebration. You are at the center of your creation: Your very own circle of radiating energy.

Choose joy. Right now, deep breath. Smile. Relax your shoulders.

Make your changes as small as they need to be. Only you will know the right place for you to make a change. Have faith. (And if faith is a little shift, celebrate the very idea!)

Writing Into Your Life

I'm going to ask you to make a shift now. This book is about changing your life, gently, sanely, to embrace your own form of creative expression. It's also about using the practice of writing to cut the path to that embrace. Gently, lightly, stepping onto the path.

Start a journal *today*. If you need a smaller shift, then make a note to yourself to buy a journal, if you need one. (Or, you can begin now by jotting a note in the blank pages in the back of this book.) It doesn't need to be expensive. It needs to be a comfortable size to write in. (Hint: I like my journals to open out flat. Hardbound books with blank pages are usually too restrictive for writing your way to creativity.) Can you pick one up today? This little act will start your imagination nodding, rubbing its warm little hands together. If you already have a journal you're using, great! Let's get started! Stay with me, I'll show you how it's done.

Take a long, luxurious breath (yes, right now!!) and write the date in your journal. Make an agreement with yourself to keep this journal for one month. Spend just five minutes in the morning making a note to yourself of some kind. (Spend as long as you want after that, but just commit to five minutes.) Write the promise in your journal. Just that. It's a little shift. Even if you don't understand how, you have begun to open up time in your life.

If you are already a journal-keeper, start a new page or invent a way to mark a new beginning point. Write your agreement to try little shifts. Say hello to your vision. Your imagination is watching. Can you feel it? Sometimes when I am deliberately engaging my imagination, I get a little fluttery feeling right above my stomach.

You are making a shift in your perception of yourself. Writing in your new journal opens the window to fresh breezes. You are joining a community around the planet, taking a rich breath of time and beginning to write the future.

Here's another little shift. Breathing deeply, treat yourself to an affirmation. Use words that work for you, something like this:

"I am breathing time into my life. With one deep breath, I change the context of my day. I am gently bending my energy toward my unique expression of self."

Light a Little Candle

All through this book you will find opportunities to choose small changes. Consider each one to be a tiny candle you are lighting deep in your soul. With the very first one, there is luminescence where there once was darkness. That is a profound change.

Your imagination, that brilliant, outlandish, willing partner to your soul's desire, will carry a torch if you will light it. As you travel through the weeks and months, choosing little shifts along the way, your inner life will take on the unmistakable glow of joy.

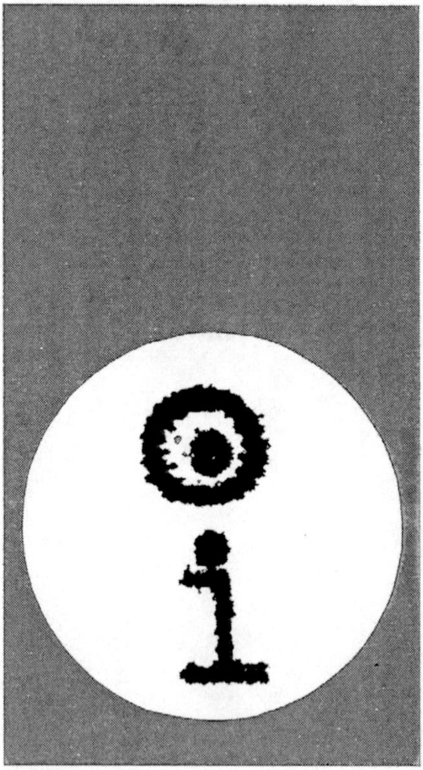

CHAPTER TWO

RADICAL ACTS

radical   --*adj*. 1. fundamental 2. far-reaching; thorough. 3. revolutionary.

That wily imagination of yours loves a challenge. Maybe that's why we have these deep dreams that can seem so far-flung. Dreams such as, say, a hunger-free world, clean environment, loving partner, or even a little time for personal pursuits.

This group of radical acts is really a curious exploration into what our culture has become -- and what it could be, with our mindful, playful participation. Take your time with this chapter. Making notes as you read gives your imagination a chance to speak.

For most people I know, life in the mainstream culture has become a pavement-pounding thunderstorm of activity. We barely have time to think.

Whoa. Let's take one second and let that sink in. *We barely have time to think.*

If this is true, how do we experience our lives? How can we possibly make decisions about what we are doing, and what we want to do? Beyond that, what hope do we have to change anything -- to participate in any way in our rapidly transforming world?

The truth is, we *are* participating. We are playing a role that has evolved from the pressures of survival, circumstance and achievement. And we rarely ponder the consequences of the choices we continue to make every day. (If we do, we think we aren't doing enough.)

What makes my list of Radical Acts *radical* is this: Any one of these acts fundamentally changes the current course and begins to redefine the status quo. In some way, each one stands outside popular culture.

As you read over this list, some of the items may whisper to you with special purpose or meaning. Keep your journal nearby so that you can write your impressions of these things. Just jot down a few words.

Every one of the Radical Acts opens a tiny window, drawing light into your essence. Allow yourself to be informed by what you feel, without feeling pressure to change anything.

What you are doing right now, in this moment, is enough. When you discover an act that speaks to you, smile, and take a deliberate breath. This allows you to begin a shift.

Working with these acts, you may discover a bit of resistance to the process. This is another thing that makes them radical. Listen to the resistance. Write about it. You are rewriting yourself as you create your future.

Every little shift is a radical act.

1. STOPPING

Stopping gives the planet a chance to catch up with us and our free-wheeling lives.

What defines stopping? Your own inner feedback provides the definition. If you are like millions of American women, your life is packed with activities both obligatory and self-mandated. Stopping happens when you close your eyes, take a breath, and feel the spin outside you begin to slow. There is a tangible feeling associated with it.

That feeling might be anxiety. We have been conditioned to believe that only by moving constantly can we survive in our ever speedier world. Like a giant snowball charging downhill right at your back, it gets bigger all the time. You've got to keep running faster -- don't stop or you'll be crushed! This breakneck speed is not sustainable, not by our finite heartbeats or our dwindling resources.

What's important to realize is that you are creating the pitch of that slope in front of you -- and you can change it. One little shift at a time.

On the other hand, that tangible feeling may be one of relief, followed by a bit of hysteria. To be told to *stop* does make some women burst into tears.

The silence of stopping can ring in your ears, a big dark cave with a singular drip echoing in the distance. This is the sound of your intuition. It is part of that unlimited source of wisdom we all carry.

When you STOP, or even SLOW, for a moment, for a day, or for a daily practice, you effectively slow the pell mell destruction of the planet. This is radical.

Little Shift: Put this book down. For just a minute or two, sit relaxed and do absolutely nothing. (Keep breathing!) You've just lit a candle.

2. SILENCE

Silence is relative. When I lived in San Francisco, a quiet night meant that I could hear the sound of the streetcar ten blocks away. Sometimes we have to take a drive in order to get far enough from life's noise to actually experience silence. Earplugs can do the trick, too. These days we even employ white noise machines in order to experience silence. Experiment with it. You will know when you have accomplished what you consider to be a period of silence.

As anyone who has meditated will attest, the noise inside us can outstrip anything going on outside the room or the front door! Maybe this is why we surround ourselves with noise -- so we don't have to hear what's inside of us.

As you start to allow silence and moments of slowness, as you begin to invite optimism and imagination and joy into your being, that noise inside yourself will change. You are adding little shifts of positive energy, displacing the things you've grown weary of hearing inside yourself. Now you are heading toward your intuitive life. You are walking along the soft dirt path in dappled sunlight, beginning to hear your deep self. Celebrate! Breath, smile, and relax.

Little Shift: As you get ready for bed tonight, think about a place in your home that you could experience silence. Just for a few minutes -- even if it's in your closet! Remember, to consider doing something different in your life gives you the first little turn. Even before you act, you have changed the energy of your life incrementally.

You can also ask your imagination for help in simply imagining a silent place.

3. BREATHING

The rushing stress of our daily lives has had one profound effect on our bodies: We hold our breath. Breathing is, of course, a reflex. But the physical and emotional triggers that keep us in a shallow breathing pattern are continually enacted in multiple forms of stimulation all around us.

Breathing deliberately and deeply restores the element of emotional stability to our physical being. Here is a simple exercise that is used in various kinds of therapy:

Inhale to the count of four, hold the breath to the count of four, and exhale to the count of eight. I am tempted to cheat when I do this exercise, counting slowly as I inhale and speeding up for the exhale. This is something to note and smile at yourself, then try again. The extra-long exhale causes you to release the held breath completely. I find that holding for a count of four "clicks" me into a more relaxed place almost immediately. Make a trigger card (or several) for this exercise. I have one right in front of me at my desk. "In for four, hold for four, out for eight."

If you have not been taught to breathe deliberately, start working with it now. In a short time you will come to see why this is a radical act.

Little Shift: Make a trigger card to start the breathing exercise described above, or copy the one in the back of the book.

4. NOISE

We're way too quiet! Wait a minute, you're saying, you just told us we needed more silence. Not exactly. What I mean is, we need options. We need to be able to find silence. And we need to be able to make noise.

An elderly friend of mine moved to a congested little village within a village in Northern California. It's rustic, even charming, but *man* is it crowded! The majority of the people living in the area happen to be sensitive to environmental noise.

Of course, they all must live with the dumpster truck roaring in, construction saws keening, sirens, car alarms, and all the rest of civilization rumbling amidst them. But something odd has happened -- these people have decided that the human voice is also not to be tolerated. They want SILENCE, and they want it 24/7! They want tiptoeing, whispering between the buildings, no parties! No singing, no laughing!

I have noise sensitivities too. But I realized, visiting my friend, that this sometimes get carried too far. We are not meant to be silent, to hush our cries of joy and exasperation. I believe that lusty singing, laughter, calling out to one another, is natural, healthy, and necessary. Quietly sneaking through our days restricts our expression as surely as it tightens our shoulders and freezes our necks.

Little Shift: If you live in an apartment or similar situation, consider how quiet you are expected to be. Give a big, loud sigh now and then. And do sing at the top of your lungs, in the shower and elsewhere! Is there a local choir you would enjoy singing with? A place you can do a little stomping now and then? How about improv or amateur theater? This is expression. In the 21st century, it can be radical.

5. EXERCISE

No single thing addresses more of our life difficulties than regular exercise. If you are in your 40s or older, you have lived with a decades-long onslaught of information about exercise.

You, like me, have likely been disgusted with the changing winds -- being told that you have to maintain a wicked pace for 45 minutes to do any good, then ten years later being told that's not true. It's enough to drive you nuts.

It took a long time for the data to accumulate on all these different exercise regimens. One thing is certain, it is better to get some exercise than none at all. What has encouraged me, and kept me out there trying to increase my fitness year after year, is the recognition that even a thirty minute walk every day makes a big difference in your overall health. You only have to try it to see for yourself. It helps.

The difference exercise makes is all-encompassing. In Chapter 6, I'll talk about having a healthy brain, and you will see what a difference we can make in our ability to keep our minds and memories intact by instituting daily exercise.

It is this expansive nature of exercise that makes it radical. It can change everything in your life.

Little Shift: If you are not currently doing any regular exercise, get out for a short, pleasant walk today. Smile, swing your arms, and experience the weather, whatever it is. If you are exercising regularly, try adding breathing exercises to your regimen.

6. IMAGINATIVE PLAY

Deeply engaging the imagination is one key to developing a positive future. And here's the fun part: *Playing* takes us to our depths!
You only need to watch a child "at work," absorbed in a world of their own creation, to see the limitlessness of our imaginations. All kinds of strange and wonderful things occur in an imaginary world.

Imagining a world is genesis. To have the best chance of discovering real solutions to our challenges, we need to be able to employ our fully developed and fully present imaginations.
How do we do this? Playing is one way. The imagination thrives in an environment that is both *safe* and *stimulating*. Our culture commonly eliminates these two essential features well before adulthood.

Translated, we adults don't consider playtime to be necessary -- or affordable. But we pay such a price for our failure to play!

Let children teach us. Watching a child, you can remember that the imagination is best at playing. Play leads to creativity. Creative solutions come willingly from our playfulness.

Our spirits take on new life when we take moments from our routine and give them over to abandon, to silliness, laughter, goofing with family and friends, simply letting time get away from us as we feel our hearts beating with pleasure. Later, we can direct our creativity. But for now, find time to play.

Playing with children, family and friends is revolutionary.

Little Shift: The next time you pass the toy store, park the car and go in -- just for you. Look around, soak up the idea of fun, find something small that makes you happy. Just window shopping can remind you that your playtime is important. Or, bring home a favorite childhood movie to watch. If you need to, see it as an assignment rather than an indulgence. Relax into it, and your imagination will join you fully.

7. USING INTUITION

Have you ever left the house thinking about something you should have brought along, something obscure, perhaps? And then the palm-to-forehead slap later that day, when that one thing would have made all the difference? You've heard the voice of your intuition. We all have. Some of us just have a more direct route to it.

Stopping is the first step, followed immediately by listening. Then you begin to discern between impulse, so often externally driven by the economic machine, and the knock-knock-knocking inside which is you, your essence, your guide and the map to your life.

Using your intuition makes room for your inner wisdom. It builds upon itself naturally, once you've begun to listen. You literally invite your inner self to participate in your day.

You will realize after the fact, with great satisfaction, that the afternoon went well because you acknowledged that voice inside. The next time will happen even more spontaneously, and soon you will develop a habit of listening to yourself. Most of us talk to ourselves, running our anxieties and anticipation through a dress rehearsal, but not many of us actually listen!

Your intuition is a key to your inner life, and that makes it radical. It can direct you to what is truly important to you instead of what the consumer-driven culture tells you is important.

Little Shift: On that bathroom mirror note, write: *I am listening*. Say it out loud during your bath.

8. MEDITATION

Meditation has so many benefits it would seem to address everything. Perhaps it does. Before you read further, take a breath, smile, relax, and remember little shifts.

Shifting towards meditation may be the most profound thing you will ever do for yourself. Just trying it, just playing with it represents a little shift. You will not be disappointed in any effort you make that leads to meditation. Of course, you can see how meditating embraces other radical acts like stopping and silence. Any one of these acts can lead to the others. This interconnection is the beauty of little shifts.

Listed here are some of the known benefits of meditation:

Mental clarity	Reduction of stress
Elevated focus	Relaxation
Easier learning	Enlightenment
Enhanced creativity	Greater stamina
Self-understanding	

Meditating is like taking silence to an extreme. The marvel of meditation is that it can be done in the midst of cacophony. But this takes practice. You may find a chance at silence by visiting your local meditation group.

Little Shift: Take yourself to one meditation meeting and just experience the silence in whatever form it comes.

9. WRITING

What's radical about writing? Well, ask any writer, it can feel pretty radical to get a piece of writing done. There's a simple reason for this. Writing requires that you take time for yourself. You begin to reclaim your desires. You act on your need to express yourself. You act with intent.

This is a formula for revolution -- definitely not supported by our culture! Once you've entered the powerful place of expressing yourself with your language, doors begin to open to other forms of expression -- painting, dancing, singing, starting your own business -- you name it. You claim it!

Karen G., a woman with a small data processing business, wanted to begin to discover her imagination. But when she sat down to write, she felt completely blocked. After a few attempts, she started a *no way* journal.

"I had no focus at all, and I knew there was no way I could express myself. But the moment I started writing, just jotting down some thoughts from my day, I felt closer to the artist inside than I had my entire life. So I wrote about that. (I cried a lot at first, which confused my husband.) But it was a gift to myself, and it seemed bigger than that even -- maybe a gift to the world. I wondered how it could be so important. Just me, writing in a journal. My best friend followed suit, and now we write together sometimes. I know my journal was the turning point.

Right now I'm writing some thoughts about a business that would make environmentally safe kids' toys. I feel like my life is bigger, roomier somehow."

Little Shift: Have you started your journal? Take a moment to greet your inner writer in your journal. Start a journal tonight. Just casually jot down some thoughts. Say hello to yourself. This act opens the door to your creative life. What may come next?

10. OPTIMISM

Optimism is the great mental state that opens the doors to potential. It is a joy-related experience. It is attitude in its most radical form.

To believe that our world can be better goes against all the media-driven slush you hear and see every day. Yet without optimism, our spirits have little reason to carry on. With an optimistic outlook (even if you have to wear it like a jacket until it becomes a real part of you) we begin to radiate our personal expression back out into the world. Many of us have put up a protective shield of cynicism after being profoundly disappointed by our culture or our expectations of life.

Remember, cynicism is a kind of emotional luxury. We can't afford it. Nothing comes after cynicism.

Disappointment and despair are ingredients for apathy. However, you can carry optimism along even in the presence of negative emotions. They don't necessarily exclude one another. You can try on your optimism and see how it feels. Enjoy a moment of faith in our enormous abilities. Breathe. Smile. Relax.

Little Shift: Here's an exercise to invite optimism into your life. Turn your thoughts toward some upcoming event, maybe a child's graduation or wedding, a work review, or the return of a friend from a trip. Picture the event, with you in it, and see the details that make it perfect for you, such as the weather, music, or smiles and laughter. Hold a picture of this moment in your mind. Now, specifically ask your imagination to help you bring optimism into your life.

11. CONNECTING

Each time we make contact with each other, we create the opportunity for expansion.

Our deep personal growth comes with interaction, working to understand each other, and having the goal of productive relationships.

The expansion may be in the form of greater tolerance, appreciation of diversity, an opportunity to exchange ideas, or simply to feel connected to our community.

So much happens when we make real connections with each other. We deepen our self awareness and our awareness of our shared humanity. Self-esteem grows.

Connecting comes in many forms in the 21st century. The Internet has been thought by some to isolate us, but that is a choice we each can make. We can plug in and dial up to our Internet servers with the choice of connecting across towns, states, and continents.

Don't be afraid of what we call virtual connections. The Internet as it exists today is both a product and a tool of imagination. This technology can greatly speed positive change.

Little Shift: Relax with your journal for 20 minutes or so, and jot down your concerns, ideas, or desires about community and connection. Would you like different kinds of relationships?

Are you finding a place to be heard? We all need many different kinds of support and interaction. Find some time this week to check your local bulletin boards or newspapers for ongoing groups that might work for you.

12. ASKING

Asking is a doorway to self-discovery. When did we unlearn how to ask? Somewhere along the line, our culture taught us not to. As an independent, self-sufficient woman, I tend to resist asking for anything. Actually, I'm terrible at asking. I'm afraid that, for some unknown reason, the power will go out, darkness will descend, and I'll end up having to clean all the spoiled food out of the refrigerator, because the universe will shout an unequivocal "NO!" in response to my asking. Still, I'm learning to ask. I started by asking my own imagination to help with the task.

Asking requires that you layer in through your personal onion, finding the needs you have at each new layer. As you ask and then listen, your dreams bubble up, and they are needy little buggers! It's time to ask for all that you desire.
Maybe asking feels superficial, like all you can think of to ask for is a new car. Go ahead! Practice. Pay attention to what it feels like to ask. Who are you asking? Can you allow yourself to need the world? To need your sister, your friend? Try to ask without expectation, there's a good trick. Just ask, simply. Asking is different from expecting.

When you ask, you tug on the universe, telling it to release abundance. You give us all permission to have needs. You teach us how it's done.

Needing people is a form of competence.

Asking really means breaking your heart open to the love and desire that runs deepest. This is what makes it a radical act.

Little Shift: Ask a friend to help you with something. Do you feel like you're intruding? Like no one really has time to help you? Go ahead and feel that. Ask anyway. Make it something small and fun this time, like helping to bake cookies. Next time, graduate to asking for help cleaning out a closet.

Notice how your connections to friends and family grow and change when you ask for help or guidance. Are there some people you should not ask for help? Are there others who are just waiting for you to ask?

13. CANDLEPOWER

Most of us have had some kind of experience with power shortages. Many states have had rolling blackouts, along with the news of corrupt politics where power sources are concerned.

Depressing, isn't it? The use of power and the business of selling power are deep issues touching every area of our lives.

We are subject to forces beyond our control all through our day. The alarm goes off. We turn on the light. Take a hot shower. Make coffee, get the cream from the fridge.

Blow-dry hair. Listen to the radio. Turn on the news and -- woops, stop that one!! Then we start our cars and hit the gas station on the way to work. Where does this put us, exactly? In a powerless existence. We are absolutely subject to the powers that be -- the providers of fuel and electricity.

Candlepower is a concept that helps us break from the supreme reign of power suppliers.

Power outages are perfect opportunities to experience silence, stopping, listening -- *candle power.* The delivery of power to our plug-in lives is an issue we are going to grapple with for a long time. In parts of the country where electricity or fuel means survival -- because of extreme weather -- we can experience candlepower during the milder months, or in smaller stages.

We can turn off the lights -- and the TV -- a little early one evening. Spend a little time in the glow of candles. Does this seem radical? My neighbor has two teenagers. He is a writer, and his wife is a self-employed human rights attorney. I met him on the street the other morning, and we talked about how our evenings go.

At his suggestion, I went out on the street to look up at his house that evening. Every room was lit up bright as day.

He explained the typical evening to me. "No, we don't actually watch TV, not much," he said. "Both kids are online, separately, from the time they finish dinner until they go to bed. I'm usually working on the computer, too, finishing up something from my day. My wife sometimes dictates tapes for her assistant to type up, or she reads."

I asked him what he thought about taking a break from their routine one evening. He laughed, but he said he'd talk to them about it. Later that week, we met downtown. He came over to me, beaming, and gave me a hug.

"We did it!" he said, "we turned everything off!"

I was surprised. He was so skeptical when we talked about it, I figured he'd just forget about it.

"No," he said, "I told the kids it was *radical*, so they were slightly interested. My wife was excited about it too, so we agreed on Thursday night. After dinner, we cleaned up the kitchen and then turned the power off at the electrical box. My son thought it was important to 'kill it at the source.' At first, we wandered around the house looking out windows, until it got completely dark. It was so quiet! We lit candles in each room. After about an hour, we all ended up downstairs in the den. We had agreed we'd all do whatever we felt like, but I guess being in the dark just made it more appealing to be together! And we ate all the ice cream, since the kids were worried it would melt. It was like a little vacation. I went to turn things back on after two hours, like I had promised, but the kids wanted to go a while longer -- they were enjoying how different it felt! We finally turned everything on again before we got ready for bed."

In energy talk, candlepower means *strength of illumination*.

Little Shift: You can use candlepower without shutting down your whole house. Just turn off TV, computer, and lights for a couple of hours. Call it camping! It's also a chance for stopping and silence, or to dust off the acoustic guitar.

14. JOY

The advertising-driven culture of consumption we live with every day is great at one thing: Trampling the delicate little violets of joy that carpet our lives.

The consumer culture does this in a peculiar way -- by making us think that it has joy to offer, if we will only buy the next thing, the bigger thing, reach for more status, believe their message that consumption equals joy. None of us believes this, but we buy anyway, out of habit, or perhaps because the images put before us are so terribly alluring.

We cannot live balanced lives without recognizing joy, taking it in some form like a delightful, healing medicine, every day. Joy lubricates our essence and generates optimism.

Devote moments to joy. When you make your list for the day, try including a deliberate time, place, or activity that allows you to experience joy. Make a date with joy. Close your eyes, breathe, smile, and ask your imagination what summons joy in your life.

Little Shift: Here are a few suggestions for joy from other women: Notice things. Really *look* at nature around you. Really look at a child's hands. Look from your heart. Look through special photographs, make a joy album where every picture makes you smile. Get out your favorite music and remember why it strikes so deeply. Let yourself laugh fully, without restriction, loud and long. Have orgasms, lots of them! Be silly. Encourage silliness in others.

15. REMEDIATION

In the language of sustaining life on this planet, remediation is a healing practice. We benefit from performing remediation in the same way that we benefit from caring for the elderly, protecting our children, or volunteering.

What makes these things radical acts is their healing nature. Every act of remediation changes the world.

During the power shortage in California, a friend told me she accidentally left her lights on when she left home in the morning. She was angry because she worried about it, and then realized "I'm just one person! I'm not causing the power shortage!" She didn't want to have to worry about not doing her part during the crisis. I realized something, listening to her. Our little efforts at reducing consumption have a much bigger impact than just the bottom line on the electric bill every month. We are asking for something when we conserve. Expressing our buying power as consumers, we also teach our culture to place a higher value on resources.

Anything that helps our planet to breathe is remediation. This could be a simple garden that you maintain, teaching someone to recycle, going online to find out if the products you buy support the environment, planting trees, consuming organic produce, writing your congressperson about an environmental issue.

Small efforts are little shifts and constitute radical action.

Little Shift: The realm of remediation is a wonderful place to employ your imagination. Breathe fully, close your eyes and imagine a clean, green planet.

The first and most important step to the creation of a healthy future is finding it in our imaginations. Starting to use your imagination's muscle is a heavenly little shift. Next, breathe, and imagine time with several other people, people you love or love working with, all imagining this world together.

Having read about these radical acts and entertained them as profound shifts, are you developing a feeling for what makes "the big difference" in *your* life? At the top of a journal page, write "I WOULD CHANGE". Take twenty minutes to brainstorm the life changes and world changes you would reach for. We each have our own creation, and our imaginations know exactly what is radical in our own lives.

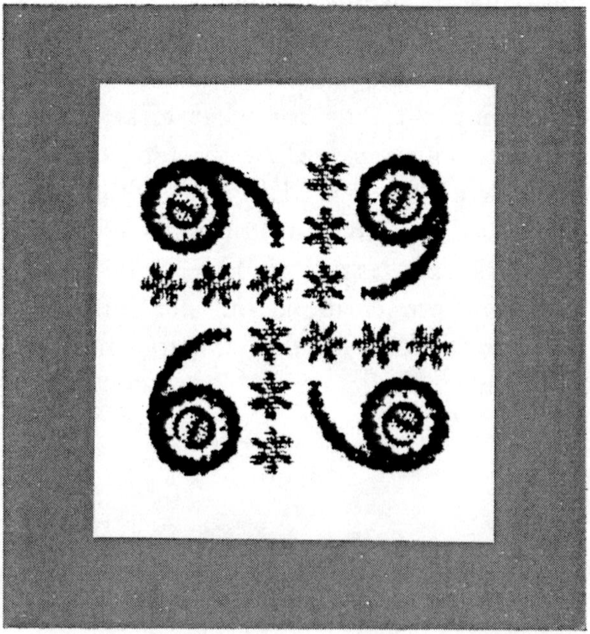

CHAPTER THREE

YOU ARE HERE

A gulf stretches between what we do and what we want to do. As life's demands increase, the gulf grows more daunting.

What does the average American do, daily, weekly, yearly?

Well, start with providing an income. We work a lot. We have friendships we try to maintain. Our homes demand ever more attention, cleaning, maintaining, stocking. Do the laundry, shop for groceries. We try to stay fit, go to the gym, walk with a friend, or at least we read articles about how we *should* be exercising! We watch television, listen to books on tape, answer e-mail, check our messages, our cell phones and our pagers.

Just the basics of day-to-day life consume most of us completely.

Daily dreams continue. We'd like to have more time with our loved ones. We'd like to do a little volunteer work. We'd like to travel, start a garden, have a child, pursue a passion. Learn a language. Take a painting class. These desires ebb and flow, but they don't go away. When we find we don't have time for any of these, our disappointment can turn to depression, despair or rage.

The price we are paying for our complicated lives has as many snaking components as Medusa. A visual manifestation of this price comes to us in the form of waste. Waste isn't just the empty egg carton and peanut butter jar. Waste is also your tired body on the couch at night. Waste is the pile of plastic toys, hardly used, the appliance in the garage that broke two weeks after you bought it.

Credit cards allow for purchases with no thought process. A lack of accountability, or more precisely, a lack of accounting, keeps us in a kind of self-imposed darkness, removed from the real activities of our lives: our personal transactions. This year I received a catalog of useless items, literally advertised as "things nobody needs." This is life as we know it.

Our lifestyles have us running to the store at every turn, wasting our time, our patience, our precious fuel, to buy products we don't really care about and may not even use. This profound waste is drowning culture.

Brighter Possibilities

Let's look at a different scenario. What if you found that you could buy the things you need from a company that was helping to clean the environment? What if your purchases were connected to programs that house and clothe less fortunate people, helping to bring them to a productive and healthy place in our society? What if each purchase and each activity had a complex connection, to a healthier, more vibrant future? How would that feel?

In my research for this book, I looked at the options for consumers. Many companies offer more environment-friendly items. But I still felt we had not embraced the whole picture. While organic cotton, for example, is a vast improvement over the devastatingly toxic production of commercial cotton, it cannot yet be produced in the quantities needed. It seemed to me that we needed more creative solutions.

Luckily for all of us, the book <u>Cradle to Cradle</u>, by William McDonough and Michael Braungart, was released in 2002. The book is a brilliant beginning to understanding the complexity of life on Planet Earth. The authors articulate the concept that just "cutting back" is not necessarily good, and may be detrimental in its own way. Recycling, for example, long heralded as the only responsible thing to do, has a downside. As the authors of this book point out, recycling is often "downcycling," reducing the material's usefulness and integrity with each change. Solutions evolve as we collect information. This requires patience and attention on our parts.

I knew the choices had become more complex. How could I give my readers a path toward the best choices? What lifestyle changes could I recommend that were realistic for our busy times?

Since I believe that our premium resource is the imagination, I wanted to help my readers make daily changes toward their facility with imagination. And that means having time. I could see that it was not productive for each individual to spend her time researching these complex issues. I wanted to give you answers.

We all must understand that the answers keep evolving. This is natural. This is good. Using our imaginations will help us tolerate and even perpetuate this healthy evolution, this constant change. In that light, I offer these suggestions as you gently change your buying habits and choices.

As we progress, no doubt we will discover that some of our choices did not directly serve the goal of a healthy future. If we can tolerate this learning curve, however, we will arrive. Mistakes are where the information surfaces.

I highly recommend reading the book <u>Cradle to Cradle</u>. The authors have produced a surprising, important and comprehensive stream of information related to choosing a healthy future.

And keep in mind the goal of this book: to trigger a voluminous surge of imaginative lives around the globe.

Now back to those consumer choices. This is daily living, and we want to be as effective as possible as we find our way to Eden.

Creative challenges await all of us in the search for a healthy future. In Chapter 10, "The Great Adventure," I discuss creative avenues for healing our lives and the planet at the same time.

Working with a Memory

Take a little time with your journal now. Think back over the past month or so. Do you remember going to the store to buy something specific that you needed, and coming home with an empty or disappointed feeling? Maybe you had an unpleasant encounter with someone along the way. Write from this memory, and change it to something positive. Write about how you would like it to be.

Now you are using your imagination to change the future.

We can begin from this moment, from this lifestyle and all its pros and cons, to change the way our future will unfold.

As you think about the directions your lifestyle takes you, consider the element of choice. In some areas, we have too many choices, and they are distracting energy drains with no reward at all.

One example of this unnecessary distraction of choice is found in your grocery store. When I began to explore the world of choices now available to consumers in this country, I had something to talk about. And talk I did. All my friends got tired of hearing it! So I'll just tell you this one thing: Our local grocery store has 316 varieties of non-alcoholic carbonated beverages to choose from. THREE HUNDRED SIXTEEN choices. And yes, I counted them. I also counted the sauces, plain bottled waters, oils, mustards, and other condiments. Every category held a shocking number of choices. I remain curious about this phenomenon. Is it an example of our great creative extravagance? Or is it just wasteful? When is diversity nothing more than indulgence, or a wasteful marketing plan?

It's something to think about. In the meantime, here's a little shift that could free up some time in your life.

Little Shift

Make a master grocery list with specific choices rather than general notes. Write down everything you know about what you're going to shop for. Not just "juice," but "organic apple juice." Write down the brand if you know it. Jot down every item you can think of that you have previously made a choice, specifically, to buy. When you go to the store, follow the list closely. You have taken the realm of choice and made it work for you, rather than the manufacturer, who hopes you'll be so bewildered by the choices that you will buy the latest new splashy advertised thing.

Impact

As you live your daily life, the impact you have on the planet's future can be loosely equated with the impact your choices have on your own life. For example, if you're a busy, run-run-run type, choosing one evening each week for low-tech, calming or contemplative time could have many positive effects (such as lowering stress) on your life, while it also lessens the stress on the planet's energy sources. Let's look at it positively: what are you already choosing that has a positive impact on your imagination? What choices can you add to enhance your connection?

It simplifies matters to see that the criteria you use for joyful, imaginative days is the same criteria that supports a healthy future!

The only criteria I can wholeheartedly recommend is to make choices that ease the frenetic pace, lighten stress, and invite joy into your daily life. For the goal of strengthening the imagination's role, these are good indicators.

Remember, life is mostly maintenance. With every choice you make, every item you purchase, you are also buying a future of maintaining it. Even if you store it and never see it again, you pay for the space in which to keep your stuff.

Choosing News

Today's typical mainstream media is inflammatory to the point of irresponsibility. We have more important things to do.

When we turn away from the constant drain of spoon-fed consumer culture we deprive the vulture of its lifeblood: our energy and our heart -- and we make a choice to feed and reinforce positive futures.

We can say no to incendiary media, quite easily. Evaluate your experience by listening to your feelings as you read news or watch it on TV.

Little Shift: Check the list of alternative news sources in the appendix. For one day or one week, try a different source.

PLANETARY PRICE:

Expensive has a new meaning. Look closely at what you pay for. Are you happy it was so cheap? What exactly made it cheap? There are planet-safe ways to pay less, and there are planet-killing ways as well. The clearest example of planet-safe is buying something that has already been used. Used clothing can be cheap or expensive, depending on what the seller calls it! Is it truly "vintage?" But this is still a great thing for the planet. Breathe easy. You've avoided the planet-expensive process involved in producing new clothing.

Notice that this is different from recycling. Recycling often involves toxic chemicals and a degradation of the original material which was not designed to be recycled. Reusing, however, keeps the material in circulation.

Having a wardrobe party is an excellent way to soothe the planet with community, laughter, and warmth of exchange.

A Guiltless Chocolate Choice

I eat chocolate. I know I'm not alone in my indulgence. Chocolate is the most consumed confection in the world.

Whenever we as a nation consume something in mass quantities, there arises a great opportunity for planet stewardship.

A few months ago the local paper ran a big article on the chocolate plantations. Somewhere on the African continent, children are, today, being kidnapped from their families and forced to labor in the cocoa fields. This detail of our global economy raised my blood pressure and lowered my mood to a dangerous level. I eat chocolate. I'm not an addict, but sometimes, yes, I need chocolate. Now what was I going to do?

According to the article, the problem is that chocolate is purchased through brokers. Early in the line of middlemen, the information is lost as to who has conscientious cocoa farms and who does not. The chocolate manufacturers don't know where their cocoa came from. So now how do we choose?

One possible answer is to know the company you purchase from. If you cannot find adequate information about the policies and practices of a food manufacturer, keep looking. The Internet makes this research incredibly simple. In this instance, I found a company, Rapunzel, based in Europe, who knows exactly where their chocolate comes from and explains what they stand for in detail on the inside of the candy wrapper.

Rapunzel is involved with sustainable foods on several levels. Concerning their chocolate, they work with special farms in Jamaica where they have set a new standard for labor.

No guilt there. Further, Rapunzel uses their own process for sugar they call "Rapadura." The details are available on their website. The process results in a sugar that still contains its nature-given nutritional value. Rapunzel is also organic, and holds a special place in the European economy.

Suddenly, my desire to eat chocolate without feeling guilt about crimes against humanity had turned into a celebration of planet-conscious business! If you want guilt-free chocolate eating, buy Rapunzel. (See Resources Lists. Rapunzel and other companies using organic chocolate are listed.)

Can you see how this applies elsewhere? The past few years have seen a big argument among organic growers, who have their own certification for organic which many growers far exceed, and the corporate foodmongers who want to use the word organic even on genetically engineered foods. Honest labeling was at stake. What a hullabaloo!! Much wailing and gnashing of teeth, "How will we know it's really organic?"

The answer to this is so simple it hurts. Companies with integrity simply label THEIR food products, informing the consumer of the details of production. No GMOs. Organic "in compliance with..." whatever organization is currently respected.

As the consumer, you simply do not buy anything that is NOT LABELED. Problem solved. Big companies, get on board. We are not as dumb -- or as silent -- as we used to be.

Little Shift: On your next grocery run, spend a few minutes in the organic aisle. Compare some brands. Take one item that you eat regularly, and switch to a brand that is, at least, organic. I say *at least* because many small organic companies are being bought out by corporate giants, and while they may still qualify for the term "organic," the farming practices are in question. Huge organic farms end up being monoculture, which is not sustainable. Treat this issue like the ongoing puzzle that it is: We are in the process of demanding a new level of responsibility for practices related to food production. It will take time to understand what the criteria must be and how to arrive there. Be patient, stay informed, and participate. The Resources section lists companies that work to keep us abreast of these issues.

Looking at Possible Futures

Observant writers are recording their ideas about what our future may hold. In "YES!" magazine in Spring of 2000, Susan Cannon offers a representation of future views held by "Cultural Creatives" she has studied.

Cultural Creatives is a term coined by sociologist and market researcher Paul Ray, to describe people with ecological, community, personal growth values.

Susan Cannon lays out four possibilities. Each one describes an imagined scenario with possibilities related to the circumstances we already face on the planet. They range from crisis to recovery. In each scenario, community and the human vision are keys to the outcome.

Susan Cannon's writing is derived from her observations of the collective vision of millions of people. Each of us continually contributes to this collective vision. Most of us are not deliberately choosing what we see for the future. By inviting our imaginations and directing our desire, we will help shape the world we are about to occupy. The ultimate scenario Cannon describes is titled "Integral Dawn." I have included it below as evidence of what we might begin now to imagine.

Integral Dawn (Susan Cannon, 2000)

Assumption: (In the future,) Cultural Creative values take hold, coupled with system stability.

The number of people in the US with cultural creative values rises until the dominant culture is colored by it. The materialism that plagued the close of the 20th century is abating.

A general recognition of the connectedness of all things and the fragility and sacredness of all life has softened actions and decision making. Economic practices are dramatically changed, and lifestyles reflect the sustainability and simplicity ethic. Aging Baby Boomers, many holding significant wealth, rediscover the idealism of their youth and temper it with wisdom.

Community, relationships, spirituality, and neighborhood are ascendant. That trend, coupled with increased population density (which insures gridlock) accelerates a move toward decentralized work, urban villages, and sustainable communities with shared collective resources. Most people do significant amounts of unpaid work. The civic sector experiences a renaissance.

An environmental "near miss" at the turn of the century, combined with shifting social values and technological advances, accelerates a turnaround to sustainable business practices.

Growth was intentionally slowed during the transition, but new value is created in the emerging Green Economy sector. We are able to do much more with less matter and energy.

A commitment to local economies, which exist as a decentralized network, balances the economic might and homogenizing effect of the global corporations. The younger generation, fervently environmentalist, is now entering the workforce. More women and Gen Xers are in positions of responsibility, redefining work, success, and progress, and redesigning organizational structure. Lifestyles, education, business practices, and even government policy are transforming.

This scenario may seem like a dream world. Yet, our ability to see it with our inner eye is key to moving in that direction. Allowing positive visions to occupy your emotional landscape, and sharing those visions with others, is the beginning of our bright future.

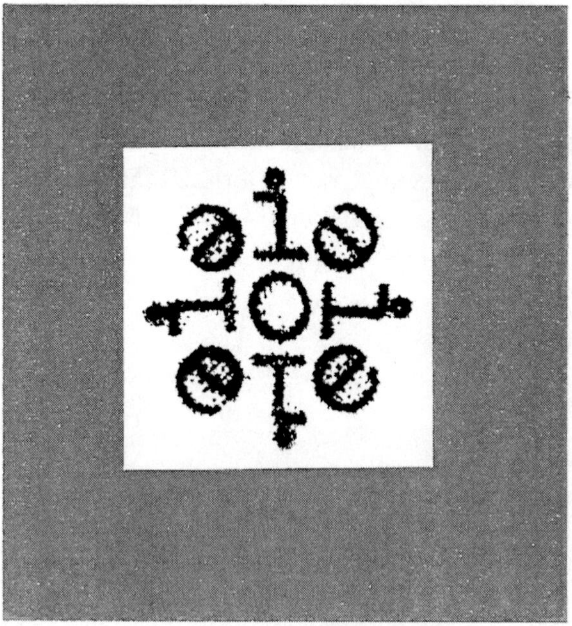

CHAPTER FOUR

CLEAR YOUR FRONTIER

A visionary life is a life lived today with a reach into tomorrow.

In order to envision and enter this life you are creating, your imagination needs an open space, like a landing pad. You may be surprised at how little is needed. The requirement is only clear space, not big space. A clear desk or table (which means you've created a place for everything that piles up on it), tells your imagination the invitation is delivered -- the door stands open.

As I write this, I'm sitting sideways on Molly's couch. I must confess to you, dear reader, that my desk at home, which I have escaped, is piled eight inches high with various projects. The cascading papers, books and binders threaten the mouse on my Tweety-bird mousepad.

Even the mental image of this chaos affects my work today. How appropriate that I am assigned the good work of helping others motivate through their own clutter clearing event! I am always grateful to my readers.

The Creative Person's Gremlins
Do any of the following statements ring a bell? If so, you are a person who will benefit from maintaining one clear space in your physical environment.

"I start projects and then never finish."

"I stay away from home because I can't cope."

"I'm embarrassed by my chaos and clutter."

"I feel like I can't accomplish anything."

"People always say to me, 'you are SO creative!'"

"I can't find my socks. Again."

"I love order but never have time to create it."

"I don't even bother trying to find things any more."

We live in environments so chaotic we cannot appreciate the creativity crawling around under the piles. We also cannot access that creativity. Our culture, with its manic consumerism and the weary beast of advertising, is burying us in consumables and advertising for that consumption. This runaway train derails our spirits.

Imposing order will change the flow of your consumer response. With order comes an optimistic relief, a playground for joy, and the foundation for creativity and imagination.

Without the peacekeeping work of clearing clutter, we live in service to debris management. Moving clutter out of our lives is a powerful step in recovering our essence.

Our True Landscape

The physical space we occupy is our true landscape. The daily visual, whether it is relief or assault, is the magic carpet taking us to our destiny.

At this moment, this book is being born in a claustrophobic attic flat with poor ventilation. We've been here many seasons, working our way through various obstacles of health and fate.

It takes real orchestration to live successfully in cramped environs, and I am often discouraged by the energy it takes to make it livable.

The biggest obstacle to an open frontier is the continual accumulation of STUFF. Our wasteful culture pours into our lives. The final distraction: Maintaining it all!

Help is Available

Books, articles, and consultants all can help with the challenge of creating a clear living space. But something more is needed, perhaps because we are cluttered with the debris of help itself! That something is *motivation*. In this chapter, I give you the basics of clearing a space, along with a little extra encouragement and little shifts to ease the way.

CLUTTER: TAKE IT SERIOUSLY

Imagine that you are looking for a piece of paper. It's a bit of information, a letter from your grandmother, or the instructions for your new answering machine. Now. Imagine that you know where to look. You walk to the file drawer, open it, and go straight to the folder labeled "Correspondence" "Granny" "Echo 2X11 digital". Found! You have achieved order.

Are you able to do this in your life? If you can, then you're a hell of a lot further down the road than I am!

Until very recently, as I came to care deeply about my writing and my other projects, it went something like this:

Where would I have put that thing? Daisy's vaccination papers, where, where, where? I mumble to myself as I shuffle through a stack of bills, letters, advertisements, magazines. I have an 'aha!' moment but it's because I found the cover page to a book chapter that I was looking for two weeks ago.

Dog stuff, dog stuff, it's in here somewhere -- OH! I know, I know, it's got to be in this box. "This box" is a banker's box I can't even lift. It holds National Geographics, a folder labeled "color," three boxes of Christmas cards, and a big, messy stack of papers with a sticky note on top. The sticky note has one word scribbled in pencil: *FILE.*

The stacks represent an element of my life that is out of control -- a kind of succumbing to a cultural machine. That's depressing! Further, you may be one of many who have a kind of "environmental sensitivity of the conscience" -- you see all that slick catalog paper coming into the house, and a sinking sensation follows.

On some subtle level, you may recognize the tremendous waste of this process, and know that by allowing it, you participate in the free-falling environmental degradation.

Changing this -- which opens up space in your own life -- will lift the cloud in ways you haven't anticipated.

Let's Get Started
I suggest a cup of hot chocolate or aromatic green tea, along with a cheerful friend and happy music, to ease the way.

ONE SMALL ACCOMPLISHMENT

Here's a radical act and a little shift: choose your one place to make a landing pad for your imagination. In the next chapter, we'll look at your actual creative workspace. For now, choose a spot for the exercise of making a small space. You can move it if you need to later on.

Make this spot off limits when you come in the door. Do not set your purse, your mail, your jacket, or your dog on that table. Not your keys either. Make another space for them.

This core spot is the beginning of having a place for everything. It sits there, subtly teaching, training the rest of your space how to be. Training you with little shifts.

Make a trigger card or perhaps a bigger sign to put on that clear desk that says "NOT HERE" or "NO JUNK."

When you come in the house, and you gravitate to that spot because it's the only clear spot you can see, and you see your note, then breathe, smile, relax. Keep moving. Throw your stuff on the bed or on the couch where it will be addressed sooner rather than later.

Clear this spot completely. If it's a corner of a desk, give it parameters. Use some of those shells you brought back from your vacation, small toys or other special symbols that you enjoy. Stake out the corners of the landing pad.

With this cleared spot to gaze upon, you will be more able to see the problems the rest of your space present. Do you have piles of magazines, bills or filing laying around?

Take it a little bit at a time. I use a grocery bag to throw things in that are leaving the house. One bag full may be enough for today. The trick is to maintain a conscious look at what you are throwing out. This is where you begin to understand the little habits that keep your environment chaotic. It is not easy for most of us to change this. Little shifts are important as you start to clear your environment.

Magazines are a big problem for me. My husband and I enjoy several different genres, and it's amazing how they pile up. I haven't yet been brave enough to count how many magazines come into the house every month, but it would be a good exercise. The first little shift I made was to cancel some of the clothing company catalogs. They tend to go a tad overboard. Not only do they send multiple catalogs every few weeks, but they keep a separate listing for every misspelling of my name!

I started tearing off the address section every time a catalog came in, and put them in my desk drawer, paperclipped together. After a few weeks, I had a stack of them. I made time one morning to make phone calls and have the catalogs and magazines canceled.

Take a look at other things in your space. Even if they are fun toys, meaningful gifts, or otherwise desirable, they are all speaking to you. Do you want all those voices in one space?

For cards and colorful images from friends and family, find a way to incorporate them -- minus the chaos. Try a bulletin board, but instead of tacking things up randomly, create a neat pattern with your color. I have a glass box that was used for a street jeweler's display case which I keep on the living room table. I use the horizontal rods to hang cards, art, and toys behind the glass. They are chaotic, but they are in a template of order. It's working.

Get Rid Of It?

You don't have to throw everything away. What is useful is to give yourself a view of how your space could be without all the chaos.

Start boxing things up as if you were planning to move. Mark the boxes carefully and list every single item in the box on the outside. This is important, as it helps you understand that you are not discarding things you care about. You are, at least temporarily, putting them away. For a reason. For a while.

Will the boxes fit in the garage? Basement, attic? In a friend's storage space? You need to get them away from your living space long enough to experience it without them.

After you've done this, you'll be going back to your boxes and deciding what you really want in your space. This is the first and most powerful step of clearing chaos from your life.

Take a Breather

The process of clearing quickly overwhelms me. Try working in stages. Get out your journal, and write for 15 minutes about the process. Take a walk, call a friend, or find other ways to break up this important work. One way to pace yourself is to make a weekly date for the clutter work and spend a set amount of time. This can be a most productive schedule!

Changing Over the Long Term

The shifts you make in your environment will definitely affect your life in other ways. Once you start handling, literally and figuratively, all the items you've brought into your life, your shopping experiences will change. It's work to relieve yourself of excess stuff. You won't be in such a hurry to buy little things and bring them home again.

Here are some things to think about when you are shopping. Try putting them on a trigger card, and put that card in with your credit cards. If you've reached the point where you don't really feel good about shopping all the time, take your card out when you go into a store or mall and look at it for a moment. Let it remind you that you have a rich life without buying stuff you don't need. Let it remind you that it can feel good to window shop and not buy anything.

Little Shifts: Just asking the right questions will help move energy into this process. Since clutter begins with making a purchase, try pondering your consumer habits.

Imagine you are standing in a store, holding something you've decided to buy. Breathe, smile, relax, and give it a moment.

I am bringing this thing into my life. Not just my home, but my life. I will experience it, live with it. It will be sitting there amongst my other things. Do I want to maintain it? Do I still want it? Can it be enough to experience it in the store and know it exists in the world, and smile and relax with it here?

Is it a gift for someone else? Do THEY want it? Does it serve a bigger purpose on the planet for me to buy it? Does it help an indigenous group, preserve the rainforest, clean the beaches? Is it being made by a company I'd like to support?

Responding to these questions and aligning your shopping behavior with those responses will lift a burden from your heart.

Making space in your home increases your capacity for joy.

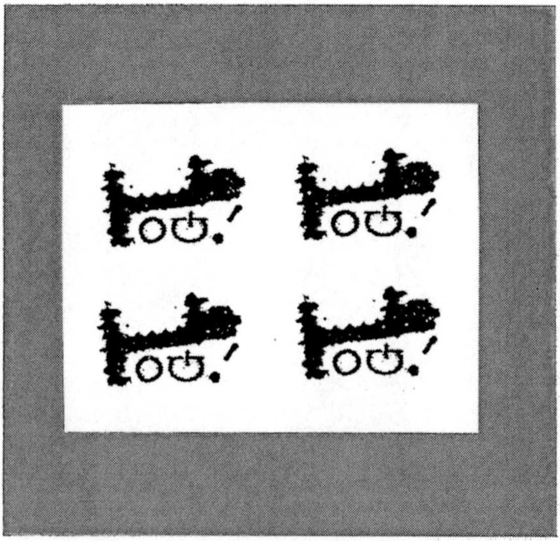

CHAPTER FIVE

THE LANDING PAD

Now that you've begun to make way for your imagination, let's look at your space for your imagination's landing pad. When you deliberately create a nook for your imagination, powerful changes begin to brew. Nurturing your imagination, the play and work that goes on in this space reinforces your commitment to creative expression.

In the process of clearing clutter, have you discovered a corner, a room, a closet, an alcove where you can stake a claim? Look around your environment again for this important space. Many of us these days don't have much room to spare in our homes.

Make this space a high priority. It doesn't have to be big. Just big enough for a table and chair, and comfortably located away from the daily household flow.

Perhaps you already have a sewing room, a workbench in the garage, or your own office. Ponder these spaces too. Can you designate part of that space for this special purpose?

Recognizing the Need

It took a long time for me to realize that I needed a spot in the house that was undisturbed by anyone but me. I have my computer desk, and a table for art projects. Both of these, however, are smack in the midst of everything else we do in our small attic flat. Once I clearly understood what was missing, I was at a loss as to how to orchestrate it. We simply had no more room!

The need for this special spot grew, and so did my frustration over our environment. My husband and I each have our personal desk space, shoe-horned into the extra bedroom or at one end of our tiny living room.

My search finally ended when I realized that my somewhat oversized walk-in closet might actually perform this function. I knew I was on to something. I stood in my closet, observing the chaos. Laundry basket spilling over, shoes everywhere. Lots of clothes I never wear. The whole picture struck me at once.

I feverishly cleared the closet. We live in an old Victorian, and the twin walk-in closets have dormer windows. Perfect to consider as a little garret!

Once all the clothes were out, I coldly sorted through them. The local thrift shop's inventory grew as I got rid of anything that was even slightly questionable. Then I packed everything that was not wearable in the current season. When I was done, I was able to put my clothes in the closet with room to spare. In fact, only about a quarter of my closet is now used for clothing.

The Garret Takes Shape

I was able to fit in a writing desk, chair, bookshelf and a lamp! And best of all, I can close the door.

I decided against trying to fit my computer into this space. It's more of a retreat. A few months later, I managed to move my computer desk into a room with a decent window. My work became more enjoyable once I moved it out of the dark hallway.

You can do this. Look around. Ask your imagination to help you figure this out, and give it a few days to enlighten you.

What Works For You?

Once you've settled on a location and cleared it for landing, bring over a chair. Sit in your workspace for a little while before you start putting up pictures and loading up the landscape. Experience it empty. Bring in a little dictionary or an art book, just one. Let the energy settle. Breathe, smile, and relax. Be open to experimenting, this is new. Your imagination will lead you as time goes on.

Now you can start practicing: Ask your imagination for guidance. This is the perfect time -- this space you're creating is for your imagination. Rest with it. Ask, before you go to sleep, "What would you create in this space?" See what happens. Write the question in your journal to reinforce your commitment.

Okay. Now, before you go any further, make a trigger card that says: BREATHE, SMILE, RELAX. Make it colorful, and put it in plain sight. You are beginning to orchestrate your future, creating a channel for your best energies to come forward and integrate into your life!
Playfulness is an all-important piece of this process. Meditate in your space for a moment on this joyful allowing. Create a mental invitation.

Start to gather images that appeal to you. Literally ask your imagination for feedback. Put them in a folder for now. Photographs, artwork, colorful toys are all great. Do you like colored lights? Or, a small lamp with a colored bulb? Photos of family and friends smiling out at you are always excellent. Also, look for images of activity, such as birds in flight, sky, clouds, or water, a tricycle parade, anything that is moving.

Pay attention to the subtle messages of your images. Do you have a little collection of gleeful ecstasy? That's the goal. Giggling, smiling, dynamic colors.

When you have your collection rounded out, sit in your space again and look through the folder. Hold up the images here and there, next to the wall, on the desk, wherever you think they may go. If something you have is an absolute, meaning you have no doubt that you'll use it, go ahead and put that up. Take your time, and be willing to change these images as often as your imagination desires!

To enhance the boundaries of your space, you might use a bead curtain, or make one of fabric or paper. It's amazing how much difference it can make to incorporate this simple little trick.

A folding screen to cordon off the space is also a wonderful idea. You can paint or decorate it, or leave it plain for serenity.

If you're lucky enough to have a window in your space, you might hang a crystal in it to catch the light. Rainbows that come through these crystal prisms are a delight to any imagination. Another fine addition is a simple, playful mobile. Some of the ones made for small children, with simple colored discs, are often the best choices. They also tend to uplift a small space.

Indulge your senses in every possible way in this creation of your imagination's home base. This is where you will come to recharge, to ask for help, and to connect with the imaginative process brewing inside you.

Little Shifts: Perhaps you are in transition, getting ready to make a move. Don't wait to create your landing pad. If you're not sure of the best spot, or you know you like to move around your space and have variety, you can start the process by making a portable version. Use an old briefcase, a small suitcase from the thrift store, or a box about the shape of a briefcase with a full lid that comes off. It should sit comfortably in your lap.

This will be your portable landing pad. Take those same images, just use the smaller versions. Special post cards, colorful things you've collected. Make an "insert" for the lid of the briefcase, a clear sleeve to hold your changing images. If you want to, just glue your images right onto the inside of the lid.

Sit in a chair or on the edge of your bed with your portable landing pad in your lap, lid open. What things call to be included in this space? Do you need special pens, pencils, and paper? A small dictionary or thesaurus? A transistor radio? Work on this space in short spells over a week or two until it feels like home. Realize that by investing this time in a place for your imagination, you are starting a new era in your life.

Whether you have a whole room to play in, or a portable box to carry around, this shift marks a beginning point for you and your imagination.

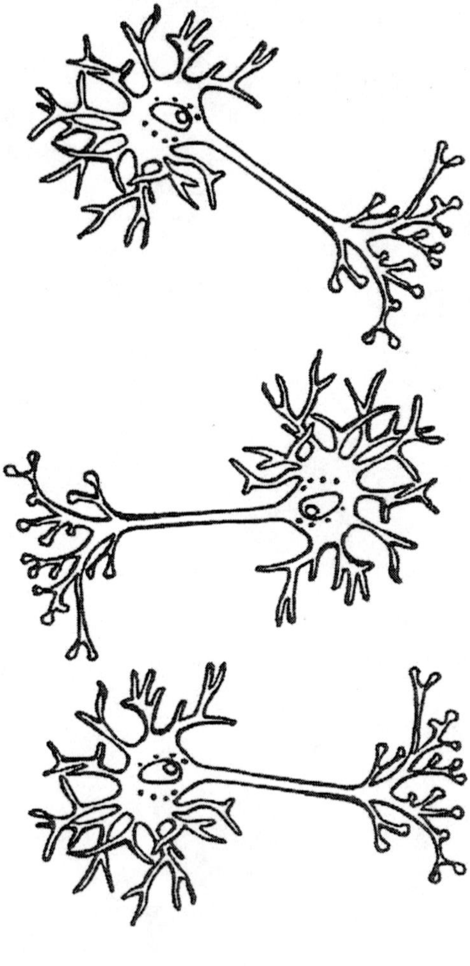

CHAPTER SIX

TENDING A WILD GARDEN

"Your brain is capable of infinite joy and pleasure. Make no mistake: the powers of the mind and memory are virtually limitless."
Dharma Singh Khalsa, M.D. in "Brain Longevity"

Imagine a garden filled with ideas. A flowering of joyful creativity. How would you nurture this special place?

Think of your brain as the garden you nourish and enjoy. Here the flowering of ideas takes place. You put your tools to work, paying close attention to the needs of this creation, unique in all the world.

Take a moment to picture this garden. Are there flowers blooming? Do you see young vegetables, a selection of aromatic herbs? Let this garden be the metaphor for your brain.

You are supplying nutrients, water, sunshine, fertile soil, and freeing your garden of weeds and damaging pests. You create the optimum environment for healthy growth. The result of all your care is a profusion of color, delightful sights and smells. The sounds of birds and bees are testimony to the connection you've created with a world beyond your own.

Here is a place for pondering, a crop of food for the next season, seeds borne and preserved for the future.

This little garden exists only in your hands. It flowers uniquely in your care, *only through you.* Its place in the world is such that it offers a joyful respite to other creatures, by its very existence. It returns your spent energy a thousandfold, in many unseen ways.

These next few pages outline the most critical components of brain health. Only you will know what changes you can make as you encourage a thriving, robust environment for your brain's health. Remember that each small change you can make has a ripple effect which leads to a greater capacity. Be sure to see the little shifts section at the end!

Use the garden metaphor to help you remember these basic components to growing a healthy brain:

For Plants	For a Healthy Brain
Clean air	Breathing & Exercise
Nutrients	Foods & Supplements
Fresh water	Filtered, 8 glasses a day
Weather Protection	Lower stressors
Sunshine	Laugh, play, community
Healthy soil	Neuron-building mental challenges

What follows is your "short guide" to keeping your brain working at its best. As you read these suggestions, look at how they interconnect. Little shifts in any area will benefit all aspects of your healthy brain.

BREATHING AND EXERCISE

Breathing designed to assist brain function is an orchestrated exercise of its own. The two following exercises are also employed in yoga techniques. As you work with these, imagine the increased oxygen dispersing to all the cells in your brain. If you tend to have headaches, for example, it might be helpful to see the oxygen as snowflakes, noticing the intricate detail of the crystals. If you are someone who is often cold, a better image to imagine could be a warm gold glitter nourishing your brain cells.

Slow breathing: Inhale slowly through your nose, filling the base of your lungs. Hold the breath for a second when your lungs are full. Breathe out slowly, from the top of your lungs down, through your nose. Focus on your breath.

Rapid breathing: This exercise increases your energy. It may seem like hyperventilation, but it actually increases oxygen in the body. It will make you calm and alert.

Breathe in and out through your nose rapidly, faster than one breath per second, without pausing. Keep your chest relaxed and focus on your navel area. Some people use this exercise daily instead of the afternoon candy bar or cup of coffee.

Exercising: Twenty minutes a day will make more difference than you can imagine, especially if you are not exercising regularly. Make a trigger card that says: YOU MUST GET UP FROM YOUR DESK. Follow it. If you work in an office and only get 10 minute breaks, use them to walk quickly around the building or up and down the stairs. Try to bump it to a full thirty minutes. A thirty minute walk every day has been shown to have dramatic results in keeping weight off, relieving depression and sharpening brain function.

FOODS

Certain foods are highly recommended for brain health. Begin slowly, adding one or two foods or supplements every couple of weeks. It is more effective to add beneficial foods than to try to stop eating ones you indulge in. The less helpful foods will be edged out in time.

These are at the top of the list for brain health:

Fish, especially salmon
Cruciferous vegetables such as broccoli, cabbage, and cauliflower
Lots of fresh fruit, organic whenever possible
Green teas and black teas
Separating carbohydrates and protein makes for easier digestion. To promote alertness, eat protein first. To relax and get sleepy, eat carbos first.

SUPPLEMENTS

The easiest supplement to include is lecithin, which is available in different forms and is generally inexpensive. Lecithin provides a basic component of the physiology of thought: acetylcholine. It has many other benefits as well.

A high-quality vitamin C is helpful, as is blue-green algae or spirulina. Co-enzyme Q10, also called "CO-Q10", is commonly suggested to relieve forgetfulness. It has many other attributes. Siberian ginseng is another supplement that assists healthy brain function.

ABUNDANT WATER

Yes, you've heard it before. Our bodies need eight glasses (8 ounces each) of fresh water every day just for basic functioning.

If you exercise or live in a dry environment, you will need more. Start in the morning with one or two full glasses upon arising and you're already ahead of the game. Don't skip this one.

Learn about the water supply where you live. Even if it is "safe" city water, you should be informed about the plumbing into your home. If there is any question, filter your water, and keep it fresh.

LOWER STRESSORS

You guessed it: BREATHE. SMILE. RELAX. Do it now.

I focus on positive things to include in your daily life, rather than suggesting that you eliminate things. When we are trying to stop doing something, we tend to focus on it with all our might.

However, in this instance, I must inform you of a real danger to your health. Hydrogenated fats directly affect your brain. The fats quickly become rancid, and this is stored in your brain cells! Avoid ALL hydrogenated fats!

Read the label before you buy. It will say "partially hydrogenated" oil, or sometimes "fully hydrogenated." It is used because it is a cheap option for the manufacturers. Don't buy it. Look instead for products that state clearly the type of oil they use. Look for non-hydrogenated safflower or canola oil in the ingredients.

Think of it this way: Would you pour rancid fat on the soil for your plants? Of course not! Don't do it to your brain. There are plenty of foods available now with better oils to replace the ones you've been using that have hydrogenated fats.

Meditation may be the single most productive goal for protecting your brain. Start with a class, a book or a tape. Introduce yourself to this important tool.

In your daily routine, find ways to decrease repetitive high-stress moments. Examine your job, your goals, and your home life to find the high stressors and write about them in your journal. Allow solutions to arise by asking your imagination for help, then letting it go.

PLAYTIME

Laugh!! Laughing produces endorphins, increases your oxygen circulation, and stimulates other positive hormones.

In Radical Acts, we looked at playing. Keep finding ways to increase your playtime and your contact with friends and family away from stressful environments. This is a powerful realm in your life. Seek out optimistic friends. Avoid movies and television programs that provoke a stress response. Stop watching the news!! Instead, start going to amateur theater productions, or have one of your own. Go outside. Have picnics. Play in the rain. Do puppet shows. Seek joy.

MENTAL CHALLENGES

Before you continue reading, TAKE A BREAK. Get up, stretch, breathe, drink a glass of water. (I mean it. Get out of your chair.)

Now. The neurons in your brain need a certain kind of stimulation in order to grow stronger and make new connections. To do this, take a new tack. Do what you don't normally do.

For example, if you are sedentary, take a dance class. If your daily work is labor, study a new language. Make sure you enjoy the new activities! It should not be drudgery. Learn a new instrument. Study other cultures. Write, draw, and juggle. Ride a bicycle.

Volunteer! Evidence continues to grow in testimony to the health benefits of offering your services to your community. This benefits you directly, as the challenges you encounter stimulate neuron growth.

Distraction: Why do so many vibrant adults in our culture spend so much time in front of the television? We need the distraction. Start planning some away-from-TV time today, if you know it's a challenge in your life. Other activities will give you so much more of what you're looking for. Moving your focus to something different allows your overworked brain to shift gears and creates a deeper sense of relaxation and satisfaction than the passive brain status of TV. In contrast, meditation provides yet another form of brain relief, more like allowing a machine to cool in idle. All of these forms of tending the brain are akin to cross-training. The new connections create ease as well as strength within the brain's neural web.

Little Shifts: Take a moment to relax. Now, imagine these neurons in your brain stretching to meet each other. Look at the drawing of your brain neuron, how the branches are complex like a healthy, growing plant. Imagine your neurons lengthening, reaching for connections in response to the electrical impulse of your thoughts. Your new thoughts -- your struggle to understand a new language or a new friend -- these provide a physical inspiration, a mandate to your brain cells, to strengthen, multiply and diversify. Eleanor Roosevelt said "Do the thing you cannot do." This is exactly what builds neuron connections.

Go back over the items I've listed for brain health. Think of all the things you're already doing. Good! Take a luxurious breath, smile and relax. Any one of these things will make a difference. If you want to speed up your ability to use your mind effectively, start with one item from each category and make a little shift toward that end.

Look at the Radical Acts chapter again. All of the acts described are great for the brain. Have you considered meditation? Yoga or tai chi? Bringing one of these practices in, starting with one session per week or even once every two weeks, will shift you toward a successful brain-health regimen.

To help you take small steps toward a fitness routine, here is another little shift. Let's say you are interested in yoga. Find a video at your library, borrow one from a friend, or pick up one at the local health food store. Sit quietly and watch it first, passively, just letting the images in. Watch ten to twenty minutes of the video. Now, turn it off and close your eyes. Breathe. Smile. Relax. Imagine your body doing these exercises. If you want to, watch a little more of the video. To maximize the effect of this exercise, go out for a short walk when you're finished. Just allow the idea of your body doing this new thing. This will help you move toward it in a joyful way.

Just as a garden thrives with the intelligent planting of varied species, your brain grows healthier when you vary your mental and physical activities. This reliance on diversity is woven throughout all of nature, including our healthy human lives.

In the same way that plants creatively evolve in their own interest, your uniqueness and your pursuit of your unique dream, benefits the world garden.

A Note to Future Elders

We are the elders of the future, all of us. Whether you are 34 or 74, you are already impacting the future. You can choose your future impact, starting right now.

What are we choosing today for our own personal health? Whatever the answer is, that is also what we are choosing for our whole culture and the future of this planet.

We have such potential as mature citizens! We have the past to refer to, all our experiences to bring to the table as we create the future. But the outlook for those of us now in our 40s and 50s could be grim. Alzheimer's and other diseases continue to be a major concern among aging populations.

A positive future depends upon all of our diversity. Your life experience is a precious source of wisdom that we cannot afford to lose. Please start now to reclaim the years that lie ahead.

We can choose an active, joyful, productive future -- or we can become a massive population of zombies. We are choosing right now.

CHAPTER SEVEN

IMAGINE IT HERE

Little shifts and radical acts are two great tools to help you steer into your essence, making room in your life for your imagination to fully blossom. In this chapter we will explore tools to bring your imagination forward and integrate its gifts into your life. You are creating a powerful ally.

The past four decades have seen a steady avalanche of information about "visualization." Appropriate techniques abound for creating a mental picture of what you want. Visualization is used for everything from healing cancer to finding a new career. (It works pretty well for finding a parking spot, too.) It is clear that to start the process of bringing your dream into the world, you need to create a *picture* of your desire in your own mind.

Let's get started with playfully inviting your imagination to come out. The following exercise will be used in different ways throughout this book. Remember, even as you read along, you can start engaging with your own imagination. Keep your playful spirit for all of these exercises.

Your imagination is made for joy.

Visualizing

Have you ever tried to get a mental picture of your future? Sometimes my students say "I'm not very good at visualizing." I think we are all masters at imagining -- it's just that we have not consciously directed the process. *Choosing* the path of your imagination is a different experience. If you are new to this process, allow yourself to just read along, and stay very relaxed and casual about it.

Take your shoes off. As you work, if you notice a little excitement showing up somewhere in your body, (toe-tapping? head-scratching?) take a breath, and smile. You're already making the connection! Relax and allow it. Remember, whatever *your* style is, it is just perfect.

Starting to Imagine

Let's take a few minutes to establish a creative exercise that you can use throughout this book. This is a simple, fun way to engage your imagination and practice visualizing at the same time.

Sit quietly and comfortably. It's best to keep both feet flat on the floor if you can. Close your eyes and picture a blackboard. When I do this exercise, the blackboard is a small, old-fashioned slate board with a wooden frame. Yours may be green or gray, or some other image. Let your image emerge as it wants to. Next, make sure the blackboard is completely clean and clear. Mentally erase it if needed.

Breathe comfortably as you allow words to appear on the board, calling to your imagination to wake up and say hello. Allow sensory information, too, such as a soothing tone to your voice as you call to your imagination. The more senses you employ, the more engaged you are with your inner self.

Continue to view the blackboard, seeing your words appear there in white chalk. Let the colors change as they will -- this is your imagination interacting with you!

Try saying "Yoo hoo! Hello in there! Imagination, hello!"

How does it feel to call to your imagination? Do new pictures appear? Keep breathing as you experience this in your body.

You may actually hear a response. I have. As I continue this work to summon my imagination, the experience of it grows richer.

Remember, your imagination is the most playful part of you. It is pure, undaunted joy. Of course we all know that we can imagine really horrible things, but even this is evidence of the intense creativity inside us. Recognize this rich resource, and have faith in it. You can steer your imagination's energy, taking you wherever you wish to go. Let's continue.

Picturing the blackboard now, allow it to recede into the background. In front of the board, or next to it, however it occurs to you, make a place for your imagination to actually reveal itself.

You are now summoning the deep, special part of you that is completely original. Your imagination is the culminated mandala of your life, your personality, and the collective experience. Sit quietly and enjoy the image that surfaces. It may not be visual at first. You might get a body sensation, a warmth, an ache, even an annoyance called "Nothing's Happening." Just acknowledge, allow, and observe yourself in it.

When I made contact with my imagination and saw it for the first time, I was being led through a light self-hypnosis. I was stunned by the display as I called my imagination to appear. So many facets to the picture!

It is hard to describe on paper, I need to use my hands! Remember Cousin It from the Addams Family? This character was about four feet of walking mop-string hair. My imagination looks a bit like that, except that every strand of hair is gleaming and glittering, a rainbow of colors, with Fourth of July sparklers flying off in all directions. It spirals and gyrates and crackles with energy.

What does yours look like? You may feel like you're "faking" or forcing a visual, or making it up. Don't worry! You are! That's your imagination, happily handing out images. With a little practice, you will come to know the patterns of your creative process, and the images will be familiar. Use the image I described if you like. Your own imagination will change the details.

HINT: When you picture your blackboard, if you find that the chalk letters are annoying or tedious, that's your imagination wanting to give you more. Try seeing a picture, like a movie screen, instead of the written words. Experiment freely with this imagery. Evidenced by our dreams, our psyches use pictures, not words, to communicate. For some, the words may feel safer or more accessible, for others it's not enough.

Everyone's imagination will have a different need for variety and expression. For example, some of us are more excited by drama while others enjoy extreme subtlety. All of these things are testimony to our uniqueness, our originality: the imagination at work.

Allow it all to surface while you breathe, smile, and relax. This clears the highway for your imagination's pink hovercraft limo, complete with solar panels, to come cruising in.

Your connection to this rich resource is something you can choose. Choosing it means you are plugging in to the place where all your questions about your life will ultimately be answered. And a whole new batch of questions formed!

Use this exercise often. Write it out in your journal or use the list at the end of the chapter to trigger your memory. Keep returning to this. As you repeat it, it will become a part of you in a way completely unique to you. It is a tool for your life.

Navigating Your Sea of Potential

What if you just don't *know* what you want? The place called Not-knowing is a rich wonderland to explore. However, this floating, vague place of uncertainty can make you feel lost. If you are traveling through the vast potential of your life right now, this powerful little exercise can help you navigate. With this exercise, you will practice the art of observing yourself.

Take a luxurious breath and exhale. Smile. Relax.

Imagine yourself sitting in a comfortable chair in an empty room. Imagine the air cool or warm, however it is most pleasant to you, with pleasing light coming through a nearby window. The air is fresh as you breathe deeply, sitting quietly in this soothing space. Allow pleasant sounds to surface, the sounds of water, birds calling gently, or music that calms you.

See yourself enjoying this place. Your eyes are closed, your hands comfortable in your lap. Keep watching yourself sitting in the chair. As you watch, see yourself becoming more vibrant, as if something is occurring to you. Energized by some thought, you watch yourself.

You do not know what the idea is, but you can see how it changes your appearance. Perhaps you are sitting up straighter in the chair, or looking out the window. Are your eyes open wide? Do you see an open, excited expression on your face? Keep observing. What is happening now? Perhaps you laugh or exclaim, or clap your hands together.

See the energy in your body as you observe yourself now knowing *exactly* what to do. Watch yourself stand from the chair and stride from the room, utterly inspired and excited.

Let your imagination work on this one. Allow the uncertainty, and just imagine yourself making discoveries. Realize that before you reach

that place of knowing, your possibilities are the broadest they can be!
You are literally training your mind to allow your imagination's power to surface. With the positive excitement of uncertainty, anything *can* happen.

Imagine Faith

Faith is a tricky concept. I was raised in a Protestant church in which faith came first. We were basically ordered to accept it. I remember being taught in Sunday School a cliched old lesson. The teacher, a thin middle-aged man in a brown suit, asked us to stand. I stood with my fellow six year old mates, mostly looking at each other's shoes. "See that chair behind you?" We nodded, "yeah," looking up at him. "Now sit down." We sat like trained bears, still watching him closely. "Why did you sit?" he asked. "Why did you trust that chair to hold you up? How did you know," he said, very slowly, "that that chair would not just collapse under you?" My brow furrowed as I tried to follow his logic. He narrowed his eyes and pointed a long finger at us in classic evangelical style. Truth about to be revealed. "That's faith. You had faith that the chair would hold you up." He leaned on the table behind him and folded his arms, looking at each of us with satisfaction. I raised my hand. "Um? I had already sat in my chair before, so I knew already it was okay." I waited for a more detailed explanation of the process. As usual, the teacher was satisfied that there was only one smart-aleck in the group, and he moved on to Bible study, having made converts of most of us. I went home with a new image in my little head, and carefully checked all chairs before I sat down until my parents asked me to stop.

Faith is not such a flimsy carnival trick. It is woven into hope, depth, experiences that we carry through our lives. It is vulnerable, easily betrayed when we are disappointed or grieving. It is valuable, worthy of pursuit. When I imagine faith, I see a small child running. She's got the stem of a daisy in her fist, and she's running because she can. Her face is wild glee. In that moment, she is pure faith, the kind that arises from innocence. This is one form of faith we might have before we begin to recognize the world also contains darkness. Adult faith often must be reconstructed out of some intangible form of energy we find within ourselves. This is where imagination can help. If you care about someone or something in your life, there's your starting point to nurture faith. Begin with a picture of this loved one in your mind. As you sit quietly, allowing this image, observe your feelings. Does something inside you feel like confidence in this person? Engage with this feeling, and ask your imagination to show you other examples of faith. Observe the mystery of it, the cultural wrappings, the stories and history attached to this idea. Go gently if you have lived with cynicism, or consider yourself jaded. Faith is a kind of flood within. The supply is vast, and there is no need to hurry.

If you consider yourself a person with strong faith, let your imagination bring you information about faith in a positive future, faith in other people's potential, and faith in your ability to find your deepest form of expression.

Little Shifts and Journaling

Now that you have started to wake up your imagination, use your journal to enhance the process.

Play with a different ink color, or make colors in your journal pages, outlining them with felt tip pens, using stamps, or cut color from magazines and tape in.

Take one blank page and create a frame for your words. Write something silly, like "don't forget low-fat at corner store" in the frame. Enjoy your unique handwriting. Interact with the visuals that you create by building on them.

And when you're through with this, write a short paragraph to your imagination. Tell it how much you enjoy the offerings it brings.

Ask your imagination a question in your journal. Write it decoratively. As you do this, you are engaging your imagination in the very process of communicating with it.

Your Journal As Home

Treat your journal as your imagination's safest place, a realm of unconditional acceptance. Use it as a celebration of originality. Describe weirdness, craziness, deep need surfacing, allowing all to unfold in this faithful confidant. Using your imagination fully is how you participate in the creation of our culture.

*There is a vitality, a life force, an energy, a quickening
that is translated through you into action,
and because there is only one of you, in all time,
this expression is unique.
If you block it, it will never exist through any other medium and be lost.
The world will not have it.
It is not your business to determine how good it is,
nor how valuable,
nor how it compares to other expressions.
It is your business to keep the channel open.
You do not even have to believe in yourself or your work.
You only have to keep open and aware directly to the urges that activate you.
Keep the channel open.*
--Martha Graham

Rama Vernon, in the book <u>Fabric of the Future</u>, tells us:

"When the moments grow between each thought, Vision begins to appear. We may receive it as an idea, an impression, an inspiration. It arises from the field of collective thinking, a gene pool where ideas originate and perhaps even return."

Imagine Yourself with Energy

I have been working with, around, and through chronic fatigue for three years. This book came through it. But it wasn't until I was almost finished with the book that I hit on this discovery -- the idea of imagining myself with energy. Try it. It's a whole new world.

Sit quietly in your imagination invitation mode. Breathe. Smile. Relax. As you relax deeply in your chair, feeling your body's weight being supported, breathe and exhale fully. Allow an image of yourself at your best. You're wearing clothes that feel like you, comfortable and active. Now picture yourself walking outside, swinging your arms, in an environment that appeals to you. What is the temperature? The sounds? Picture your feet moving strongly along as you walk. Add an incline now, and stride up it without slowing. Your breathing is deep and powerful. You've reached the top of a hill, and you stop here. Reaching your arms out and up, invite your deep effervescence to emerge. Feel the warmth in your palms. Notice the clarity of your sight. Allow other details of strong, healthy energy to coalesce into this vision. Breathe, smile, and relax as you bring your vision back home. Ask your imagination to continue to add details of this energy image tonight as you sleep.

An Imagined Guide

The following is an imagination adventure from my journal. As I worked with my imagination, continually asking for more, this magical genie was born. She birthed herself, emerging from the cocoon of her own making.

She appears in the form of a giant cocoon, floating above me, ten feet high, mummified, wrapped in a gauzy glory. I can see her breathing. I can feel her smile. I relax into the rhythm of her.

The cocoon rumbles, rips and splits, and I see the ribbon of darkness appear for a second from top to bottom, the edges of the split curling out like giant lips.

Peering into that dark slit, I'm suddenly knocked back by a lightning shock of neon as thousands of butterflies, a riot of fluttering color, orange, hot pink, lime green and turquoise flood through the opening.

The cocoon is effervescent, glittering gently as it disappears, revealing my genie again, the butterflies resting, slowly opening and closing their wings, an entire cape of them surrounding her.

She smiles, silent, beaming benevolence at me, abundance, pure possibility, and love. We enjoy a long, pure breath together. The butterflies are organizing into a spiral pattern, a checkered rainbow moving deliberately, musically around Genie.

I recognized her as a magical manifestation, teaching me the joy of engaging my imagination. When I feel low or "dulled out," I can go to this image and hang out with it. I am building a sort of portfolio of inner resources for myself.

Writing Exercise

One of your best guides in life is the inner resource you create: the connection to your imagination. What would your guide look like? Write for 20 minutes, using words to sketch an image of this helper. Remember, it is a pure projection of your essence. Ask your imagination to participate. Write quickly, it is important to allow unedited details. Your guide could be anything or anyone or any combination of your life's experiences. Allow surprises! Borrow my genie if she appeals to you, then change her into whatever is best for your needs.

Using Color, Pattern and Texture

Bringing stimulating color into your life and your environment does not require going out and spending big bucks on framed prints or paintings (although masterful artwork is a wonderful way to enhance your space).

You only need to orient yourself toward a more colorful existence. Keep in mind that you are not only trying to create a stimulating world around you, but more importantly, you are responding to inner signals about color and imagery that will feed your creativity and awaken the desire in you to reach further still. Thus you begin a kind of dialogue with your inner world that results in a fully expressive life.

Most of us already decorate our work spaces to some degree. Now, take it to another level. Wherever you spend the bulk of your week, begin to bring more visual evidence of your deep symbology into that space.

For sources of pattern, texture, and color, try going to the thrift store. Scarves or neckties often have stimulating patterns. Or, use construction paper, old fabrics, wild color collages you've made, a big board you've painted with scarlet latex paint. Make a mandala of all your wild colors. Tack, staple or tape pieces together. Juxtapose them this way and that. Find something that makes you feel happy - we're shooting for ecstasy here -- and put it on your wall, on your desk, over your door. Mount it or prop it up. PLAY with these things. There is no real end result we're after here. There is no wrong way to do any of this.

Writing Exercise

Start by spending twenty minutes or more free-writing in your journal. Write down descriptions of colors. Does midnight blue have a feeling associated with it? What about neon green? You can make a wheel, writing colors you love, hate, find interesting, like to wear, or saw recently while driving or walking.

The brain takes in information much like a cocklebur: Thoughts wheel along, grabbing at connections in your mind with little hooks, like Velcro, like very sticky tape, picking up everything in its way. There is nothing linear about how the brain processes information. As you get comfortable with less linear writing and doodling, your creative process emerges. This leads to wilder, happier, more interesting work in your journal, and the back-and-forth process is in motion.

Always curious about the mind, spirit, and connections to language, I have used my journal as a place to experiment with a variety of language-based images. I have written large across the page, sometimes in reverse image (as if you're seeing it in a mirror), sometimes starting at the bottom right and writing up the page. These things may sound tedious or confusing, but if you play with them, you might find your imagination perking up and taking notice.

The brain is intrigued and enhanced by veering off course. I practice mirror image writing in particular to push those neurons along onto a new path.

To give you a better idea, mirror image writing consists of forming letters in reverse, starting at the right side of the page and moving left. When you stop, you should be able to hold the paper up to a mirror and read it normally.

Although the idea to try this came to me on its own, artists and writers have used this technique for centuries. Try it! It's a great break if you suffer from boredom or just not wanting to "get going" in your journal.

Pay attention to the way it makes you feel as you write. You are bushwhacking through new areas of your brain, so it could feel silly, or make you nervous, or hit your funny bone! When I am lucky enough to remember to do it, I have even used mirror image writing to break myself out of a case of the blues.

Don't forget: new neural connections, those all-important indicators of brain growth, happen when we do something different.

Spontaneous Collage

Using color and imagery to decorate your journal makes it more than a notebook you are writing in. I use discarded magazines to cut out images and colorful patterns that appeal to me.

My favorite way of decorating a journal is to start with nothing in mind, leaf through some old National Geographics from the thrift store, and cut out anything that is visually interesting to me until I have a pile of paper to choose from. It takes a while to break the habit of READING the material as you leaf through it. Try to ignore the content and just quickly tear out pages with good color or imagery. Then put the magazine aside and spread out your palette of paper.

One quick way to make an intriguing cover is to make narrow columns of color. Start cutting one inch strips out of the pages you've selected. Go quickly with it, make snap decisions. Then just line them up on the front of the journal and glue or tape them down. Or, experiment with rearranging the colorstrips before you secure them. I'm a quiltmaker, so I also am happy cutting little squares and arranging them in tight patterns on my journal covers.

I have also taped down stones, shells, string and fabric on my collages. Usually, I put tape down heavily over the whole thing when I'm done, so I don't have to worry about it getting wet. Play with your options, let your own imagination carry you along in this joyful process.

Little Shifts: Don't have time to make a collage for your journal? Just take this one step: Find a card you like, cut the image off the card and tape it to the front of your journal. Just experience "messing" with your environment in this way. Next time, maybe you'll be able to set aside a little more time for it. Enjoy!

Portable Altar

Altars have become more common as cultures merge in today's world. If these special spaces appeal to you, you might create an altar to the prowess, wildness, instinct and radical-ness of the imagination. Close your eyes and think of open doors and light coming in. Look around your space with an eye toward the altar-worthy items in your life, personal and unique. Like the Portable Landing Pad I described earlier, this physical manifestation of imagination can exist in a miniature form, on your desk, in your briefcase, or in a little box that travels.

Creatives tend to leave a trail of little altars. When I am cleaning up the house before our cleaning lady comes, I am acutely aware of all the special little messes I make. For example, let me describe my dressing table. I am looking at it right now. (Oh, dear.) In the middle is a tray that corrals my favorite jewelry. I can see from the extra piles that this week has been stressful. Crowding my earrings and bracelets are a velvet juggling ball, a tape measure, and a couple of shells. The tray is over-full, so more bracelets and hair ties are on the table surrounding it. But as I make my way through the days and weeks, I have come to see these special messes as little altars to my life. It helps me understand my own process. I embrace this chaotic part of me, and use the altar idea to transform it. Later today, because my attention has been brought to this particular mess, I will straighten it up, put some things away, and arrange the items I want to look at. This is one kind of altar. The portable altar is made of things that comfort you. I use a cigar box. When I travel, this box comes along. I take it out in my hotel room and set up my own sacred zone right next to the bed.

Writing Exercises for the Imagination

These exercises are designed to keep your imagination in the active mode.

A tried and true method of getting to the "real" writing is to write as quickly as you can, in your journal, for a set amount of time, like 10 minutes. (Don't make it too long or you'll end up with a righteous hand cramp). Write fast and furious, and most important, do not edit. This means you never cross out a word. It's that continuous stream you are trying to reach, and going back and crossing out means you are giving in to the editor -- the left brain.

Once you've tried it, you'll see how the left brain just gives up. "Fine! You don't want to do it right, I'm not sticking around to watch!" This is an uproarious success. And your writing will amaze you. Try not to get attached to this. Have fun, give in to your imagination, keep going until you hardly notice you're writing.

Here's a hint when you are starting out with this process: As you write, and you are thinking "Shoot, that's not what I meant to say," then WRITE Shoot, that's not what I meant to say, and keep going! Or write the word you wanted there, and keep going. When you get the urge to cross something out, write faster, using your pen to gallop away from the editing moment. Faster, faster! Develop a wild (but readable, you'll be glad you did), trot of a script that you can use for this kind of writing. Sometimes I just stop crossing t's and dotting i's, so I can move at a quick clip along the lines.

Another trick I've used successfully is to write in two or three word columns. So it ends up looking something like this:

when i write
i want to say
everything just
perfectly as if
i am being graded
on my own journal
and i know that's
not true but I
can't always
convince myself
not to do it.

Then I start at the top of the page and make another column. Two, three or four words in a line. It shakes up your editor mind and activates the creative process.

I like to use a few words that I call "home base." For this exercise, here are some words that describe movement. Look through them, pick some that make you really happy, and write those at the top of your journal page.

Then, glance at the clock, and write for ten minutes using these words. If you get stuck, write the "home base" words over and over. Your brain will get bored and start something more interesting, trust me. You can even write "I don't know what to write, caper, cavort, frolic, I don't know what to write." If all you do is repeat words, don't worry! Even that has a meditative quality and you will be taking a break from the editing left brain. Here's another exercise:

MOVING WORDS: Writing exercise

Take at least 20 minutes to write quickly, without stopping except to look at the list that follows. Look back on this exercise in a few days, and see if any themes arise to tell you positive direction to point your energy.

sway - whirl - shimmy - flow - fly -

locomote - swing - glide - prance -

skip - stir - caper - cavort - drift - frolic -

spin - switch - trip the light fantastic

Nature's Mystery

Nature has many tools for tantalizing the imagination. Mushrooms are an excellent example of this intrigue dancing among us. Current research shows that mushrooms play an important role in cleaning pollution from streams. It goes something like this: The mushroom "colony" grows and advances on a stream. But before it gets there, it sends out a biological form called a "crystalline entity." (I am not making this up.) This correspondent checks the stream and returns to the colony with pertinent information. For example, if the stream is infected with the bacteria e.coli, the colony will then respond by producing a "cleaning crew" which precedes its arrival and clears the bacteria from the stream before the mushroom colony endangers itself. Neat, huh?

Imagine you are these crystalline entities that the mushroom body sends on ahead. You are bringing back information about what is before us: the future! You are heading out with a task: To observe what's before you, to make some kind of sense of it, and to return with your own description. In this case, imagine it is also your responsibility to make recommendations about how to proceed based on your observations. This is a very personal task.

Imagine, now, that you are going out with others to do this work, and all of you will have a slightly different take on your findings. You will return with all of this individualized information and turn it over to be digested by the whole body. Imagine that whatever you can retrieve that is most uniquely *you* is the most helpful and most informative information. Those pieces of the puzzle that stand out in originality are the determining factors.

Do you see how this would affect the decision made by the mushroom body, this original information? Do you see how your comments that fall in accordance with all the other entities are not the crucial pieces? It is the *differences* that change the color, adding black, white, or brown, darkening the communal shade or lightening it, contrasting or blending.

Nothing in the world matters so much as your uniqueness. If you will begin to make these small turns to open the doors to your expression, the world you are creating will begin to look more like the vision you hold inside yourself.

Writing Exercise

Become aware of that vision. What are you imagining every day? Create an imaginative future in your mind that you can return to many times a day. Use all of your feelings, your daily experiences, losses, triumphs, frustrations and comfort, to create this image.

What are those experiences which stand out the most -- the bad traffic? The smiling face that makes your coffee at the deli? What are you feeling during your day? What moments bring you satisfaction, the completion of a report? Lunch hour with a special friend? Walking alone outdoors? Don't bother to judge your responses, that is not the purpose here. Observe. See what is uniquely you in it. Know this to be a necessary element in the vision you will return to.

Your Imagination is Without Limits

We act on our expectations. Our expectations are formed by limiting criteria -- unless we shift to an imaginative way of being in the world. This is the primary impact of inviting imagination into your daily process.

Imagination is an inner resource. That's why it takes stopping, slowing, silencing, reassuring, embracing to allow it to speak. And then -- entertain! Stimulate!

Outlandishness is what the imagination craves. The manifestation of creativity, full blossom, will probably look insane. The crazier the better!

Writing Exercise

Write for twenty minutes in a crazy mode, using colored pens or scrawling huge on big sheets of paper or paper sacks. Let yourself make no sense. Write crazy nonsense. Let it come through. This crazy place holds great art, great writing, great insight, and brilliant solutions. Then return to your journal and tell yourself about that process.

As you stay in partnership with your imagination, you'll expand your ability to imagine -- and with this comes the return of possibility -- the return of potential -- the realization of our dream as a whole culture. First, we need to hear about the diverse visions we can imagine. Then, we can imagine integrating our diversity into a competent future.

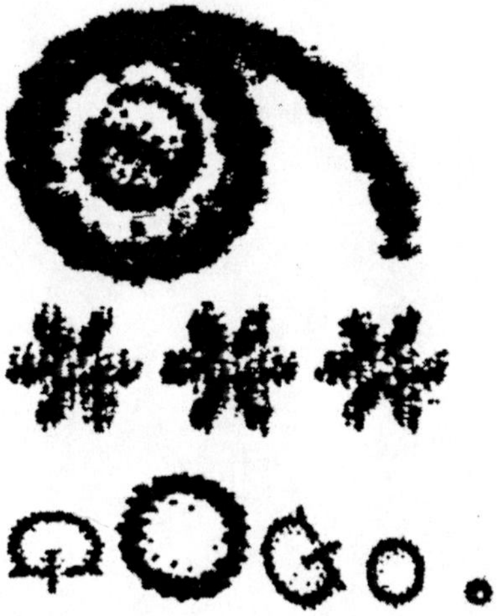

CHAPTER EIGHT

WRITING THROUGH THE WINDOW

From Suzanna's Journal
Huge releases make you wise. It is not the taking in of data, but the moment of complete dispersal. That is arriving. Giving up the flow, the accumulation of learning. Giving it away is when it happens.

This book is about holding your dream-filled life in a way that allows you to look at it clearly. As you shift your way along, budging out unproductive behaviors and adding joy, a pattern emerges. Writing regularly allows you to see this pattern. Within your journal you attend the flow of your life, noticing what recurs. Each daily session is a cobblestone in a beautiful path winding forward and back.

Finding the Time

Take a moment to consider how you can fit regular writing into your life. Step back from the idea that this project will take too much from your day. Within your journal is an energizing machine of momentum that can make everything else coalesce.

To begin this process, sit in your chosen place of creativity. The first time, don't even plan to write. Sit quietly for five or ten minutes, feeling the energy of your creative spot. Take a breath, and as you exhale, imagine yourself writing. Feel the flow of expression traveling from your heart out, down your arms, into your fingers and through the pen onto the page. Remember that this place can move with you, out to the yard or behind a closed door if your home environment is too hectic. As you breathe, smile, and relax in this place, notice how much time there actually is in a five minute stretch.

Could you broaden this out to fifteen minutes each morning? I believe fifteen minutes is the magic number. If you will commit to your writing time this quarter of an hour every day, you will begin building a solid path to your creative expression. More is better, but only if it is realistic for your life at the moment. Starting with five minutes is a good way to acknowledge your desire to create writing time in your life.

What follows is a series of writing exercises. These are designed to tug you closer to your own center, excite your imagination, and give you new ways to think about your writing.

Exercise 1: Playing With Imagination

Set aside half an hour for this exercise, so that you have time to do the "writer's stare," where you hold your pen and stare off into space between words. Things happen while you're staring. People should be paid for this necessary activity!

Get ready to write fast and easy. You are going to write as if you are telling a close friend how wonderful your day was. It's the end of the day, and you are describing to this dear friend.

Let your joyful presence inform this writing. Shake out your shoulders, take a big deep breath, exhale deliberately, smile, relax.

What do you see? Did you sleep in or get up before dawn? Did you have breakfast with a loved one? Focus on the flow of your day. What would feel good? A walk in the morning, some gardening, yoga? Late breakfast with like-minded friends? Fill in all the details just as you would like it, forget about "reality." Would you go to a carnival, play with children, go surfing? Write fast and easy, paying no attention to grammar or spelling. Let your feelings flow across the paper.

Having done this, you may get up tomorrow a little disgruntled. Your life may feel too far away from that state of perfection to even think about it. Don't be discouraged. You are already opening the door, and a sliver of golden light is coming through. Breathe. Smile. Relax. And jot down your feelings in your journal. "I'm too sleepy to write. Don't want to go to work this morning. How will I get through the day?" Your journal is becoming an ear, a place to see your life more clearly.

Opening to this process through writing may present deep unconscious questions. We are aware of these conflicts, but we tend to go about our lives ignoring them, hoping eventually they'll subside, or some magic solution will appear.

When I become overwhelmed by conflicts that I'm trying to ignore, I tend to respond emotionally, crying at everything and nothing. It's embarrassing! Looking more closely at this dynamic, I changed my mind about it. The tears carry information.

I believe these outpourings mean we are living closer to our real-ness, more tuned into the fragility, beauty, and potential of our lives.

If you find yourself sobbing, suddenly and often, try to be gentle and compassionate with yourself. Your tears may mean one or more of the following:

Reasons for Sobs, or,
YOU ARE NOT CRAZY

- You are desperate to discover what your life is for.
- You are flooding with inspiration that has not made it to the surface.
- You know the answer to a question so big you don't even know how to articulate it.
- You are having lots of thoughts about the quality of your life, and you are on the brink of putting it all together.
- You have doubts that your present life can accommodate The Real You.
- Any or all of the above, and you are scared sheepless.

Feeling confused and depressed and weepy seems to me a mark of intelligent listening. We understand, deeply, that we are completely connected to each other and to all of life, and we all want to feel better! This puts us in a quandary. Since we care about our lives, and about each other, and we want to feel better, doesn't everything need to change?

The answer is yes, and more than yes, the answer is everything *is* changing. We are the indicators of this restless, gorgeous, vivid blossoming of intelligent life on earth in the 21st century.

Exercise 2: Could Be Hormones

Write for 20 minutes starting with a description of your emotional state. Even numbness is a feeling, so describe it, whatever it may be. "I am sitting at my kitchen table (desk, the cafe, etc.) fighting tears." Write this and keep going. "This keeps happening. Is it just hormones? I'm fatigued, stressed out, frustrated, angry ..." When you allow yourself to write out the worst of your moments, your inner expression is more able to completely emerge. I make a practice of this "hormone" writing about twice a month.

Exercise 3: The Jumpstart

Gather two or three of your favorite pens. Use different colors if you like. Open your journal to two facing blank pages. Hold your pen gently above the page, then allow the point to land on the blank page like a light bird. Draw it along with a relaxed, loose hand. Let your wrist pivot back and forth as you scrawl. Doodle. Squiggle down the page. Decorate the borders with squiggly relaxed lines. Follow your urge. Allow a flower to burst in the middle of the page. Make tiny hatch marks in a long row. Use your pen rhythmically, making patterned marks. Hold the pen in different angles.

On the next page, picture the energy of your imagination flowing with the ink onto the page. Scatter single words randomly about the page.

Now write from here: 10 minutes of free, loose writing from this imagination-energy you've opened to. Write a welcome. Write an invitation to your imagination.

Room to Grow

Show your imagination you are ready to scatter the fences. Look over this list of words. Read them, hold them in your mind for a moment, then write for 10 minutes, using one or more of the words from the list.

TERMS OF EXPANSION
(to the process of becoming overjoyed)

radiance   jubilance   euphoria   keen   ample
rare   magnificent   plush   sublime
exhilarate   limitless   exult   sterling   quicken
lavish   effervescent   gleaming   spark
sagacious   gracious   rapturous   voluminous
heroic   incandescent   galvanize   roomy   wise
optimistic   paradise   infinity   mother

Establish Your Rhythm

Each of us has a unique way of getting to the writing. My book writing day often begins with a total re-invention of myself. Many writers describe this. It can be a harrowing half hour or so, where one sits with all the strangeness involved in creativity, writing or not writing, mulling, rubbing eyebrows, and adjusting the harness that is usually required in order to get any work done. If you experience this, know that you are not alone. Allow for every unique aspect of yourself to exist within the writing process -- but keep returning to the writing. Use and re-use the above exercises and word lists.

From Suzanna's Journal

If you believe in the process, you won't need to put on the brakes – or force a definition – or hurry – or fear the outcome. Return to faith.

Little Shifts: 1. If a regular writing practice seems too daunting, you can begin by asking your imagination for an opening. Close your eyes and relax. Allow a picture of yourself writing in a relaxed state to emerge in your mind. Ask your imagination to help you invent this comfortable place where you have the time and the courage for writing. Leave the outcome alone. Keep the picture free of limitations.

2. In a few days, take a minute to make a list. Quickly write, grocery-list style, all the things in the way of your creative time.

3. Use the blank pages in the back of this book to write your own invitation. Invite your imagination to offer its energy as you begin to write. Start with five minutes a day, right before bed, at lunchtime or on your break at work, sitting in your car when you come home from shopping, any time you can steal to be alone with your journal.

The Force of Your Voice

Each of our lives teach the world. A friend of mine has suffered with chronic fatigue and environmental sensitivities for many years. One day she told me she felt her life was for nothing.

"I am so unproductive," she said. We sipped tea and looked out the window at a deep redwood valley. "Sometimes I go two weeks without accomplishing a single thing."

I looked around her small apartment, taking in details of the space she has created. Simple possessions on a driftwood shelf. The kitchen floor, a soft beige swirl of earth-safe linoleum. Hemp linen dishtowels. Glass jars of organic beans and pastas. She had come to these things by way of her illness, phasing out the toxic items in her home. As I sat pondering, it struck me that she is a force on her own. Even her illness is an expression.

"Your home is a model for planet-safe living," I said, "slowly but surely you have created a living lesson. Could you write about this?"

She looked at me with surprise. I'm sure I saw a sparkle flash across her tired smile. She told me she would start working, as well as she could, on how she produced this gentle way of being.

Environmentally sensitive people are the canary in the coal mine called Earth. They have triggered an entire industry of toxin-free, earthsafe products. Paints, flooring, adhesives, bedding and toiletries are a few of the items that are being developed in response to this need. Although much more innovative thinking is needed, many of the companies involved tend toward earthsafe practices as well. Even the advertising for these products serves a bigger purpose: Bringing our attention to these critical issues. This is an example of the degraded planet speaking back through humans to remediate itself.

What is your unique message? This is the force of your voice. No matter what your lifestyle or your perceived limitations, you have something to say to help us form a healthy future.

Venturing Out

As you become more connected to your own writing, you have something new to offer the writing community. As women gather to write, a promise is carried into the culture. The next chapter is a map into one potential outcome of our writing.

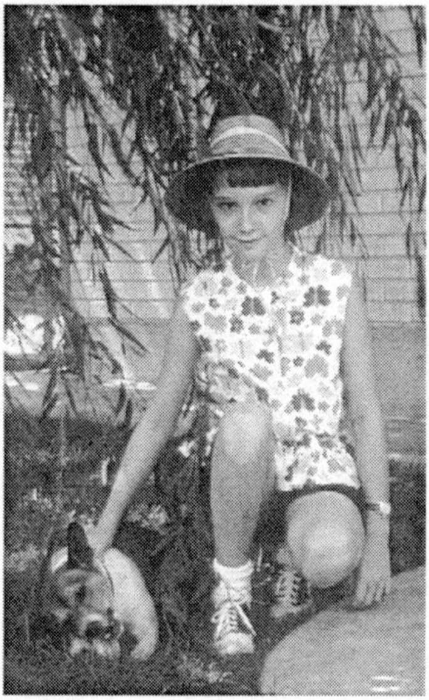

CHAPTER NINE

THE MEMORY PROJECT

A GLOBAL ANTHOLOGY

I want to connect with you, my reader. I want to understand the connections my readers are making. Where is this work of the imagination taking you?

I also intend to share this information with the global community in the form of story. To this end I have begun an anthology. Through this project I can complete a circle by publishing you. In this chapter I describe how the project works and ways for you to get started.

Our Stories

Something important is missing from our historical archives: Women's stories. For many reasons, men have had the monopoly on the printed word for centuries. Men's stories are important too, but I believe we need to address the imbalance of information currently at play. Generations of women's' lives are missing -- a huge void of guidance and insight gone. In order to create a balanced and healthy future culture, we need to embrace the stories of women's' lives. This chapter is your formal invitation to participate.

The Memory Project In A Nutshell

- Readers begin to write their stories, and then gather within their communities to write together.
- After working with the project lists in this book or on the website, these groups of women self-publish their own regional anthologies.
- The completed anthologies are sent to me. I will then select from them for a global anthology.

Positive Outcomes

Women's lives translated into stories become a template for imagining our future. Speaking together and reinforcing our common ground creates a massive force on the planet. Then, using modern technology to distribute our experiences bonds our individual future-desire into one focused direction.

It frees us from being used by technology and puts technology back in its proper place, as a tool. Another natural outcome of writing together, of course, is community bonding.

Women are emerging strongly now as leaders in the global community. Any work that we do together, for a purpose, trains us and educates us as to how to work on a larger scale.

Weaving our stories together, we strengthen our understanding and wisdom, broaden our vision, our options and our impact, and extend our flexibility and our ability to orchestrate visionary changes in this great changing time.

Let's Get Started

Writers do well with a few parameters. To that end, these topics are a beginning focus for your story writing. As always, relax, give yourself time, and allow your imagination to lead as you write. I am far more interested in where your writing takes you than the product of a rigid focus. If you have access to my website, please do visit and exchange your ideas there.

Write for 20 minutes on one of these concepts:

- What has disappeared from your life? What do you miss? Places, plants, people? A part of your ancestry?
- Future: What would you place in front of you, ten years out, so that it is there when you arrive? Imagine it and write in detail.

Detail Exercises
- List the items on your desk or dresser, table, shelf, or a crowded corner. Be sure to include colors and textures. Write from this list for 20 minutes, including feelings, in a stream-of-consciousness style.
- Take your lists to your writing group to share and write more. Is there a commonality? Write for 20 minutes about the most common items in your homes. Write about the most unique items.
- Look out a window of your home. What's out there? What is the dominant color? Can you see the weather changing? How do you feel about it?
- Spend 20 minutes detailing your feelings. Is there a warm or cold part of your body? Does it have a color? What emotions are mixed with your physical feelings? Let each part of your body speak on paper. Remember, even numbness is a feeling with details to describe.

- Write about the details of the half-hour before your head hits the pillow. What is your routine? What do you eat? What thoughts and feelings are you having?
- Take 20 minutes to write about an element of a viable future. What would such an existence look like to you? Give yourself a magic wand and allow your imagination to wield it. Write the details!

Compiling Into Story

As the weeks pass, your writing will accumulate. Pay attention to your level of interest in this project. There will come a time when you are ready to sit down and create your own story. There are many ways to do this. It could be in the form of poetry, or a kind of recipe for the future. You might want to write a short piece describing an event in your life that you recognize as a turning point. Give yourself total freedom to allow this creation.

If you get stuck, you can always visit my website for encouragement and ideas.

Soliciting Community

How do people go about finding each other within the community? The best place to start is always in some familiar context. Your place of worship, your women's group, maybe at work. I would love to hear from women who are writing with their mothers, their grandmothers, their daughters and their sisters. Most communities have a few appropriate bulletin boards where you could tack up a notice to form a group. Start with what is comfortable, and allow it to grow. My experience is that writing groups change a lot. I would have one or two women I always enjoy writing with, and then the group would get too big. Do recognize that you know what works for you. Don't obligate yourself in a way that circumvents what you are trying to do to begin with! If you find yourself in a group that doesn't fit your needs, politely retire from it and try again. I hope that this experience will be a joyful form of new connection for you.

Other options are to take a memoir writing class, contact your library, or seek out the local Literary Arts council.

Above all, begin your own writing. When you have begun this adventure, you will find both courage and options increasing.

Publish It!

Let's jump ahead to that wonderful time when you have joined forces, written your stories, and you are ready to put your group's message into an anthology.

If you or someone in your group is comfortable with computer programs, see if she can put your writings into a desktop publishing format. Perhaps you have a friendly print shop in town who will help you make the best choices.

The old-fashioned way still works, believe it or not! Type up your stories to make a master copy and then off to the copy shop. Few things in life are as satisfying as seeing your work in print.

Finally, don't forget to send me one of your anthologies! I will be waiting for the collection to grow so that I can begin the global anthology. I suggest appointing one person from your regional anthology to keep in touch with me, so that I can let you know when the Memory Project becomes available.

Little Shifts: If this project interests you, but you feel daunted by the commitment, start small. Choose three mornings each week. This works best if they are the same three mornings. Sit quietly, and breathe, smile, relax. For five minutes, engage your imagination. Imagine yourself writing, focused, completely undistracted, for five minutes. Now, take your journal and write a short passage. Just a few sentences, about anything. Remind yourself with each session that you are building into your own desire. You are learning to create an opening, rather than setting up resistance by pushing yourself. Do this as long as you need to. Trust your creativity to emerge.

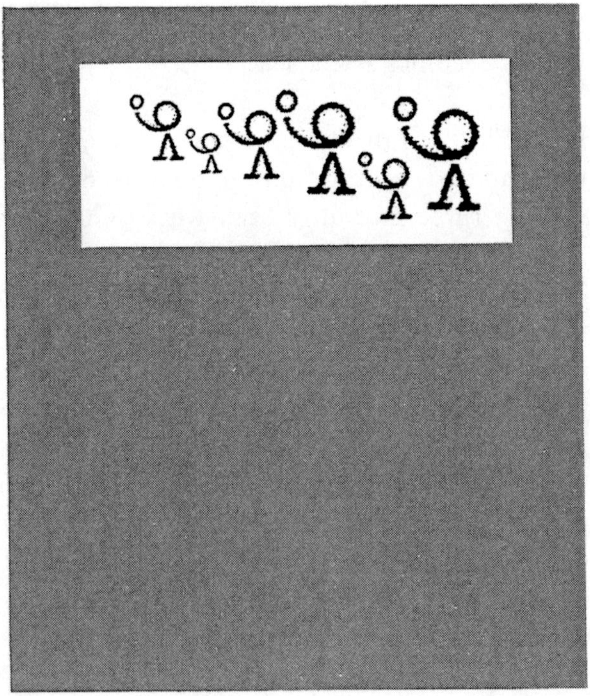

CHAPTER TEN

THE GREAT ADVENTURE

Where our imaginations go, so will we.

I imagined a book that would help people reach their deep dreams, and connect them to a bigger purpose, ultimately plugging our creativity into a tangible plan to heal our future. What you are reading now is the product of that imagining. It is one of my adventures. It has opened doors to many other paths.

The breeze at dawn has secrets to tell you.
> *Don't go back to sleep.*

You must ask for what you really want.
> *Don't go back to sleep.*

People are going back and forth across the doorsill
> *where the two worlds touch.*

The door is round and open.
> *Don't go back to sleep.*

Jelaluddin Rumi

DREAMS YET TO DREAM

My good friend Molly asked me one day, "What do you want to do with all this?" I looked at her fair, honest face. We were discussing our lives, our visions, our projects. I told her, "I want to scoop up the world." She beamed her wise smile and nodded.

Scoop up the world. It's a dream, but a vague one. What did it mean? Working with my imagination, asking for clarity, I was surprised to realize it meant specifically this: *I want to reach a million people with my message.* How could I do this? I held the question close, observing what came to me. I took notes.

Somehow, I knew that if I could touch a million people with this message of optimism, the rest would take care of itself. That matrix I created would keep multiplying. My heart, my joy, my essential expression, *my imagined world* would be moving in this physical world as it is meant to do.

Along the way, I looked for connections -- ways to keep moving closer to my vision. I looked at projects other people were playing with, noticing what was working. When you have a vision, you have to give it up to the larger forces.

Bushwhacking my way through hours and days of indecision and uncertainty, I worked. I sweated and agonized. Sometimes, I laughed, realizing all I needed to do was breathe, smile, and relax!

The greatest adventure of all is figuring out how to live together in health on this planet. That is our 21st century challenge. The first item on that agenda is coming to a global agreement of what sustainability means. Buckminster Fuller, one of our great bold visionaries, made this succinct statement of the ideal goal:

"To make the world work for 100% of humanity in the shortest possible time through spontaneous cooperation without ecological offense or the disadvantage of anyone."

THE ADVENTURE HAS BEGUN

Visionary work is being done on many levels all over the world. As we learn to integrate our imaginative lives into a positive future culture, let's honor the work that has been done and avoid re-inventing the wheel.

Talk about these achievements with your friends. Share them on email. Spread the word of positive change.

The late Donella Meadows, a respected scientist and social visionary who wrote the column "The Global Citizen," said "It is scientifically STILL POSSIBLE to survive on this planet and to restore this planet, even with the degradation and corruption at work now..."

This is a grand opportunity for the best kind of growth -- a growth of commitment, consciousness and imagination.

Working Together

The Earth Charter is a prime example of what can be accomplished when we are motivated to move forward together. It is the product of multiple cultures working together over years to bring a common vision into being. It is a worthy model to use as we look at how our own lives can begin to reflect our participation in the future.

EARTH CHARTER PREAMBLE

"We stand at a critical moment in Earth's history, a time when humanity must choose its future. As the world becomes increasingly interdependent and fragile, the future at once holds great peril and great promise. To move forward we must recognize that in the midst of a magnificent diversity of cultures and life forms we are one human family and one Earth community with a common destiny.

"We must join together to bring forth a sustainable global society founded on respect for nature, universal human rights, economic justice, and a culture of peace. Towards this end, it is imperative that we, the peoples of Earth, declare our responsibility to one another, to the greater community of life, and to future generations."

This is the first paragraph of the Preamble to the Earth Charter. Many countries have endorsed the Charter, and in the U.S., many companies, including the Sierra Club, have endorsed it. It is very enlightening to read the entire document. You can see it on www.earthcharter.org. If you don't have access to the Internet at home, don't be shy about going to your local library and asking how to use the equipment. Most communities have some kind of public Internet access today.

Using Bucky Fuller's statement as the mini-version of the Earth Charter, let's imagine what we can bring into the world as individuals accessing our imaginations. Imagine businesses that touch the world in this connected way, healing as they prosper. This, too, is already being done.

More Visionary Work

William McDonough, dean of architecture at the University of Virginia, is a man in direct collaboration with his imagination. As a matter of fact, it is his job.

He challenges his students to design systems related to industrial projects, and then ups the ante with questions about ethics and environment. McDonough and his colleagues are engaged in creating what they call "the next industrial revolution." Here is the story of one of his successes.

The assignment was to design upholstery fabrics that could be recycled into the earth doing no damage to the environment. The project resulted in some excellent capsulized information about the textile industry, such as the fact that there are more than eight thousand chemicals used to create textiles. McDonough persevered and eventually came up with a manufactured fabric using only thirty-eight chemicals, so safe you could eat it.

Here's the really exciting part: When Swiss inspectors came to the factory, they made the shocking discovery that not only was the water used in the process of making the textiles clean, it was *cleaner* than when it entered the factory!

McDonough's textile plant produces a nontoxic product that remediates the planet in the process.

Let me make a point about the human imagination now. Mr. McDonough shows us a little piece of what can be done when we optimistically proceed to use our imaginations to find solutions. What he perhaps had not imagined was that the outcome could be a leap of this magnitude, pointing the way to future solutions -- literally resetting the dial on our ability to imagine positive outcomes! The imagination's power compounds itself -- when we use it.

I mentioned McDonough in an earlier chapter when I talked about the book he and Michael Braungart authored, <u>Cradle to Cradle</u>. Their research and their commitment to explain their findings continues. If you need an uplifting hand, go to his website www.mcdonough.com, and read about the fantastic steps being taken in industry. There is a quiet revolution going on. These brilliant minds are going to work to design new ways for humans to live and work on this planet in concert with nature.

When we join our willing optimism to the community around us, invite our imaginations to the party, and deliberately choose a positive future, a great adventure begins to unfold. The possibilities are limitless.

> Be bold, and mighty forces will come to your aid.   -- *Goethe*

Trust that your vision is connected to these mighty forces. From that trust your creative life will emerge, along with the energy and understanding of how to execute your ideas.

Anatomy of an Adventure

After the World Trade Center attack, I noticed the American populace seemed obsessed with flags, and not just Old Glory. In my small northern California town, women organized to make flags for peace, and hung them in the downtown plaza. Observing the culture again as I do, I mused about the message I was seeing.

Flags allow us to tell a little story or make a personal statement without even speaking the same language. On deeper contemplation, I made a discovery.

Here on Planet Earth, we are trying to communicate. We are using the Internet, the media, our modern technology and beginning to touch each other halfway around the globe. We are even learning to agree on these very fundamental points that mean we will survive and thrive into the distant future. How are we communicating this? What could enhance and expand this communication? I kept asking my imagination for solutions.

My project called *Tokens of Agreement* is the result of this rumination. I started making these squares-within-a-square, in colors I enjoyed. I used photographs of the natural environment for the color in the center.

As I played with it, I realized that we could use these little flags as tokens to show each other that we are on the same wavelength -- we agree that we want basically the same things. I became deeply excited about the potential of such a language spreading across the globe.

I decided to launch this little project on the Internet, where it costs almost nothing yet potentially reaches millions. At the time I am writing this, the project is brand new. To see what's happening with the tokens, go online to my website (see Resources section). A little collection of the tokens are on the back cover. Remember that displaying these tokens sends a message, a visual language, saying that we

Citizens of Earth agree to the fundamental principles of sustainability.

In my vision I see people on the streets in foreign countries greeting each other, standing on street corners, discussing in their native tongue what the tokens mean. Recognizing each other in public, they have a joyful exchange.

Here is what the tokens mean in my own words:

"I believe we can live in health and harmony on this planet, now. I show my faith in this universal desire for sustainable lifestyles by displaying these tokens. To all who are oppressed or needy in any way, these tokens announce my agreement to continue the work of healing our planet culture. To any who would use their power, through ignorance or design, to harm other beings, I make this statement: We now stand for each other. We are millions upon millions around the globe, and we are communicating. "

Together we scoop up the world.

The first half of this chapter gave you some ideas about the potential of our imaginative work. Through the book you have discovered ways to turn your life gently and realistically toward your own unique form of expression.

How might you now enter this world of adventurers? How might you heal your life and your world at the same time? The place where we can touch a great number of lives is within our businesses.

Take a trip to the bookstore. Find the reference or business section and look for the books that list possible businesses to start. I advocate having your own business for several reasons.

You can run a small home business while you still have your job, if need be. You can tailor it to your current needs. Important: focus on activities that truly excite your imagination! It's also critical when considering this kind of change that you take care of yourself -- getting overwhelmed is just a setback. As long as you are working within a comfortable range of changes, you can continue joyfully, reaping the benefits of your self-expression on a continual basis.

Using these little shifts and radical acts to heal our deep apathy allows a vibrant new energy to flood our lives. When you use this energy to discover your personal expression, you invest in the future for all people.

Almost all of us would say we want to see a more balanced world, reflected in our own quality of life. Almost all of us would like to feel less guilty about some of our routine indulgences! And most of us would like to feel that we are making a difference: that we are effective in making positive changes in our communities.

Owning your own business, helping someone who is working on a business of their own, or participating in some special way in the development of small business is a great way to offer your unique creative energy to the world.

Business is where the great visionary events come into being.

For some of us, stepping into the business world may seem like a huge leap, rather than a little shift. Each of us must work at the level we are ready for. I advocate business because it provides a structure. It can give us arms and legs beyond our reach as an individual to change the world.

Getting Started
Do this exercise in a quiet space. Before you begin, remember: Breathe, smile, and relax.

Imagine yourself in a new business. Just bring into the picture some of the details, allowing the overall picture to remain hazy. You may not know what the business is or does, if it is a product or a service. Just see yourself in a work day that is perfectly suited to your needs.

Does it include a daycare area? Is it part time? Is it indoors, with a great view, or are you outside most of the time? Imagine that it meets all your financial needs. Imagine that this work makes you feel energized, and at the end of the day, you have a satisfied smile on your face. Imagine the interconnectedness of it -- that the efforts you exert have multiple positive effects on community, environment, social structure. You do not have to know the details of how this would work, not now. Just allow yourself to feel the excitement of such a perfect job, a perfect business. Your right livelihood.

We have spent decades short-changing our abilities, our imaginative capacity, our creativity. Now it is time to start expanding our capacity for joy. Now we must allow the full expression of our originality, literally unleashing it onto the world.

Little Shift Talk: "I realize there are many ways that I impact the world. I can take a moment to let my imagination speak to the infinite possibilities that await me. "

Making an Impact

When you begin to imagine how you could contribute to a positive future, you may find that you feel left out of the tech world. This is easy to understand. Technology, especially the computer world, evolves at a staggering clip. Little shifts are a great help in this realm. Even if you need to start at the beginning, know that you are among millions with the same questions and a similar skill level. I ran my own transcription service for 15 years, and I used a computer, but when I decided to end that career I realized I was seriously out of date. The optional directions you can take are daunting. I recommend starting at the beginning even if you have more than a beginner's skill. You'll build a better foundation and some self esteem to boot.

Community colleges are a good solution for catching up with the computer world. They also offer a view into many other worlds of business. Taking a one-day course to learn about the business end of something you enjoy doing can be life-changing.

Be sure to recognize how quickly we are advancing through technology. Don't feel bad about yourself if you can't keep up!

Find an area that interests you and learn how to use the computer to connect to other people in your field, to research, and find new ideas. And always, trust that the direction you choose is valued and supported. Your uniqueness coming into the world has an inherent value. Even using the computer in an eccentric manner is important as we blossom into our diversity.

Your questions as you struggle to keep up with a class may be the ones other people haven't thought to ask.

Another thing to consider is helping someone else with their new business. Check with the Chamber of Commerce, local women's groups, your church groups or school affiliations, and find out what is going on in your community. Let your imagination lead the way. Keep a very open mind and a happy heart about your journey. You are headed toward some surprising discoveries!

Trust that with continued alignment amongst us all comes greater expansion of our potential and depth of understanding.

Rama Vernon, one of the women visionaries in the remarkable collection called <u>Fabric of the Future</u>, has this to say about pursuing our unique visions:

"Take the first steps toward manifestation. Succeeding steps will be shown progressively -- not always at once. Sometimes a veil will lift, revealing the future in its entirety. When this happens you will feel a deep sense of joy, gratitude, and overwhelming love.

"Serving the global vision through our personal vision may change thousands if not millions of lives, and in turn change our world. However, it serves nothing if we ourselves are not transformed in the process with a growing sense of fulfillment rather than an empty feeling of resentment of having given too much.

"You are not alone, even though there will be times it will feel as if you are.

"It is up to each of us. As we move into the 21st century let us align with one another to bring our highest vision into manifestation. We can make personal and collective dreams a living reality. Let us work together. We are the architects of our own destiny."

Ideas, Books, People to Further Your Journey

<u>The Seed Handbook</u> by Lynne Franks (SEED is an acronym for Sustainable Enterprise and Empowerment Dynamics), is a perfect place to gain an understanding of how women enter into various entrepreneurial adventures.

Subtitled "the feminine way to create business," it is a step-by-step guide to making your life work so that you can begin such an adventure. I highly recommend it.

Group Forums

Gather within your community to discuss these ideas. Check with your library. Are there already groups meeting on topics that interest you? These ideas will lead to others.

Make Our Dream Mainstream

Another valuable exercise has to do with renaming our experience. The words we use to describe our time are powerful. We can make our dream mainstream by persisting in using the words WE believe describe what we want and what we are doing. We talk about it, announce it, quote each other and see it in print. We perpetuate the language of our vision. We draw energy away from the designs of powers-that-be by refusing to use the media's words for our time. If we want peace, we speak the language of peace. This is integral to our forward momentum. What words would you like to use to describe this time? Our media shouts "War," daily, on the radio, television and newspapers. But is that all that this time represents? Of course not. What would we like to call it? Renaissance? Transformation?

Writing Exercise

Take twenty minutes to write in your journal. Are there words or phrases you have been hearing lately that upset you? What uplifting words could replace them? What words can you think of to describe paradise? What makes these words powerful? Are you using them daily? Write your favorite words on a trigger card and keep it on your desk.

Arbitrary Agreements

Our culture is full of old agreements that have become an unlikely structure for our lives. Take a moment to examine some of these and what they mean for your life.

For example, does your lifestyle include working "full time?" I put that in quotations because what is considered to be full time in the U.S. is an absolutely arbitrary figure. The whole economy appears to function on the 9-5 work day, but I insist this is an arbitrary arrangement we simply agree to.

When I ran my transcription service, I worked about twenty hours a week. I am a speed typist, and in that twenty hours I produced more than the average typist would in a forty hour week. (A lot more.) Part of the reason I was so productive is that I was not slogging through eight hours a day of the same thing. As far as I was concerned, I worked full time.

Many employers, especially women running their own companies, are beginning to understand that the human machine can be more productive with some innovative changes in the expectations of the workplace. Not all businesses can accommodate these changes, but many can. Many would profit by doing so.

I think you already know that a "full time" week robs you of your life, so I won't go into the details of it. Instead, look at what might begin to change it for you.

Little Shift: Change begins by recognizing your desire. Do you want to work fewer hours per week? If so, say "YES!!!" out loud. LOUD. Now. Get out your journal and write that wish to yourself. Qualify it if you need to. Use positive language. Instead of "I don't want to work so much," say "I want to work less," or "I want to enjoy my life more." "I enjoy my work. I want to work shorter hours and take some classes." "I want to work 20 hours a week and spend time with my children." "I want fulfilling work." "I want creative work."

Stating your desire is powerful.

You do not need to concern yourself with the outcome. However, be present with the feelings that arise. Next, write "I will work less." Any feelings come up yet? Give them a voice too. "Oh, yeah, like that's realistic." "On whose money?" Let it all have a voice, the sarcasm, pessimism, grief, all of it -- along with the rush of excitement and deep desire. Trust me, you are changing your life in this moment.

Ask your imagination for clues. Give it time. Have faith. Breathe. Smile. Relax.

Writing Exercise

In Chapter Eight I described a writing exercise: Think about the kind of day you have in your dream life, and write it out. Take twenty minutes to do that again now. Does it feel different, now that you've considered a broader world for yourself?

Planetary Impact of Business

Our personal and business lives swing a big stick in the realm of global impact. The following are ways you can assess your own impact, or footprint, and take actions to remediate within your own lifestyle. It's an exchange. When you "pay back" the earth for the impact you create, the earth's resources will be there for you in the future.

I am just learning about an international network called The Associative Economics Network. Their name also describes their system. I invite you to begin learning about this remarkable organization along with me. Find them online at www.associative-economics.com. People involved with Associative Economics are concerned about the separation of capital from social responsibility and seek to link capital to environmentalism and social concerns. They have developed a system that includes transparent double-entry bookkeeping and a process for sharing business financials to discover our interconnectedness in a global economy. Their work is inspired by the indications of Rudolf Steiner and other progressive economists. The system moves us away from models of competition to a path for cooperation.

If you know anything about business in the world today, you know that it is based in competition. It is also based on the premise that there is not enough to go around. Some people call this a "lack-based consciousness." As we move toward sustainability, we begin to change this consciousness. Associative economics gives us a beautiful model for bringing this wisdom into the world of business.

In the Community

Have a sustainability party. Have you ever been to a Tupperware party? You know the drill. Let's look at another way of gathering and doing what is essentially group shopping while eating, laughing, and enjoying each others' company. On my website you can find lists and suggestions for creating a Sustainability Party of your own. Check it out! I think you'll be amazed at how many connections you can make through this process. You can choose to positively impact an indigenous group while buying jewelry, or educate children about living safely on the earth, or protect animals that are endangered or abused.

In considering products for the sustainability party, use this criteria: Consider the item's use. How is it made? What is its lifespan? What things are the company doing for the planet? What is the ultimate end of this item? Seeing its whole lifespan will help clarify the Planetary Price of this object.

Consider reused objects. Women are pretty good at sharing clothes. My friends often have gatherings where everyone brings all the stuff from their closet they're ready to get rid of, and, amidst much gaiety, trading them around. This is a sound earth-safe practice. Once an object has been manufactured, all the resources that were used to create it have been spent. All the toxins produced are also here for us to deal with.

That item must be given its true value and not be wasted or thrown out. Create a new use for it with minimal energy expense. Find creative ways to extend the useful life of any items you have already purchased. Consider nothing disposable.

Expensive Emotions

A common and easily understood emotion, when we start to discuss the planet's condition, is regret. It is easy to get wound up in angry discussions about the terrible things that have happened the last few decades, and how completely depressing it is. Take a moment to consider this dynamic. Where does it lead? In my experience, it leads to despair and apathy.

Rather than returning to this unproductive place again and again, let's choose forward and upward energies.

Let's consider what happens instead if we raise our energy in order to raise the planet's energy, through deliberate choices, joyful sharing of information, and the institution of new patterns. Faith-filled innovation strengthens our interconnected web.

Starting From Here
Let's begin with today. The historical perspective is limited as a tool. We have better tools: our mutual vision is the best. Women know how to clean up and set up house, literally and figuratively. Let the rules of sustainability be the framework to make it easier to sort out what's next.

We work within this criteria, and that gives us great freedom. It adds to the focus and intensifies our momentum.

Remember These Things
We can change the world by turning slightly
Business is a powerful force for social change
Feminine wisdom and imagination are being
    called forth urgently now

The imagination loves a great project
We are rushing toward a great time
To begin is enough to break inertia

Little Shifts: Do some reading about the things that interest you. Give yourself great freedom in this. Whether you like reading about dog training, famous people, quantum physics, ancient religions, computer design, or your own family history, just do some research. Go to the library and follow the connections as you read. Do some online research. Allow randomness in this.

Journaling This Chapter
After you've relaxed with a few pieces of reading material, get out your journal. Breathe, smile, relax. Write for 20 minutes on businesses you've been involved in that did not work for you. Tell yourself exactly why, in boisterous language if you feel like it. The next time you sit down for writing time, take 20 minutes to write about a local business, employee or associate that inspires you. What elements of this would you like to see expanded in the world?

Breathe
When you look around and recognize the deep chaos surrounding and informing us, choose to breathe deeply. Choose to recognize

the breadth of opportunity in it. Choose to get your hands dirty.

Chaos is an ally. An unseen order resides within it. This book emerged out of a deep, stressful chaos, the aftermath of a potentially devastating illness. Your life's chaos has a purpose too.

Again, it is your own desire, your unique way of being in the world, of caring, that dictates where your energy is best spent. This is the beginning of integrating your desire and expression with the forces that create our future.

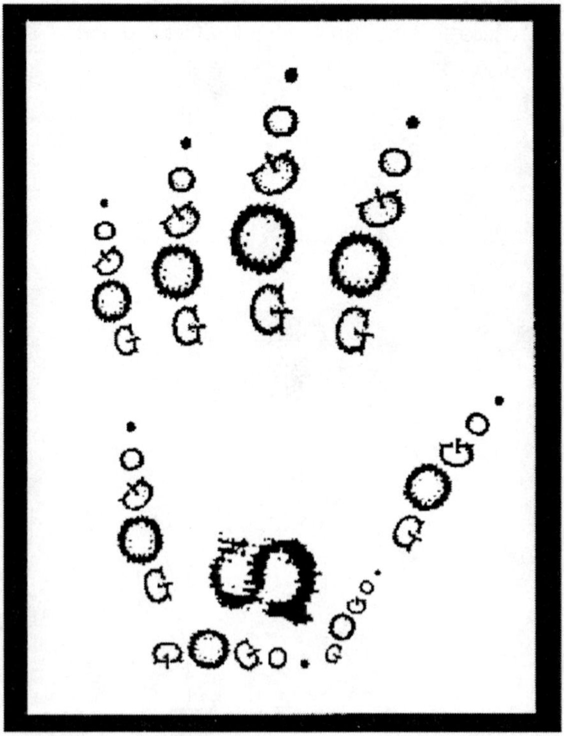

CHAPTER ELEVEN

TOUCHING EDEN

" It is up to each of us. . . let us align with one another to bring our highest vision into manifestation. We can make personal and collective dreams a living reality. Let us work together. We are the architects of our own destiny."

Rama Vernon

You don't have to look far to see a convergence of like minds here on Planet Earth. Starting from today's resources and today's challenges, what perfection can we imagine? The voices I've quoted in this book are telling us, "The battle is not over. Reason can win."

Reason can still win. If we can accept this as truth, what kind of paradise can we imagine with Reason holding the paintbrush?

"When one dreams alone, it is only a dream. When many dream together, it is the beginning of a new reality."
F. Hundertwasser

Caroline Casey tells us that complexity can be resurrected within us. She says that our circumstances of poverty, abuse, or any other symptoms of our weakened society are not really the worst of it. The worst part is the limiting of imagination that results. She says, "We need more permission, more ways of being, more tolerance." In an interview in Sebastopol, California in 2002, she asks us to embrace more art. "Yes! You're a bisexual cross-dressing cowboy scientist! Good! Good idea! More permission. Stretching the fabric of the possible. What is it to be a woman, to be a man? Let's give it a lot more room."

Entering that expansion, what can we imagine? What would we fill all that room with? What dreams, what images, what sensations?

Anxious Anticipation?

We are learning to imagine again. When you summon a vision of paradise, how does the act of imagining make you feel? Do you feel the crumbled brown debris around the edges? That's our lack of faith, supported by our perception of what has come before. I know I was taught to expect the worst. "Feeling good today? Look out," my childhood teachers said, "the downfall is just around the corner." There is this trepidation around the good experience. Surely my bubble is about to burst, gone in a flicker.

Our culture is filled with these messages. A friend's relationship starts to come apart, and someone quips "Nothing lasts forever." We are trained to bounce away from too many good feelings, back to what my mother called "reality."

"You are being so pessimistic," I would say to my mother. Then the inevitable reply: "No, young lady, I am being *realistic*."

As I read the book Cradle to Cradle, this bit of negativism from my childhood crept in. I would read the authors' beautiful vision, along with their intelligent reasoning that makes it all possible. The idea of living on a healthy planet is so filled with emotional desire it can make me choke. I sit and read, experiencing an uncomfortable blend of grief and a kind of desperate hope. I see this as the training we go through to learn how to envision radiant futures. We strengthen our tolerance of pure joy. We practice extending our arms so that we can hold this expansive vision. It's a stretch, and not a comfortable one. Why should it be? It is true growth.

So what happens when we imagine something beautiful and it doesn't come to pass? What if we see a fabulous outcome to an adventure we create, and instead something difficult happens? What happened to the vision?

I believe the images we produce have their own life. I believe we are doing something productive in the very act of imagining what we want for our world. Being ready to accept the form that vision takes when it arrives is the key to fully imagining. If we can remain open to the information within the outcome, we won't have to hold back from our ultimate desires. Instead, we are filling the future with positive energy by projecting our visions.

Think about it. We don't know exactly what happens, energetically, to our thought forms, although there are some wonderful theories about this. What if our positive visions are merging together with the heartfelt dreams of other beings around the world? What if we deliberately included this idea in our vision?

Embrace fully the brightly imagined desire. Allow this merging with other visions. You are spinning out threads, tethers that strengthen the connection to the imagination. You are informing the process with your own dream.

Accept the anticipation, too, as a tangible energy we create and move within. Anticipation allows us to reach out, grasp and transform, no matter what the seeming eventual reality. This is half of the real work available to us as humans with desires: Allowing the possibility of *good*.

When the outcome arrives, we can start there and envision again. The outcome gives us new information to work with. Now we have more clarity, more understanding of what we want or don't want, and what happens when we start pointing our desire in one direction, deliberately imagining where we want it to emerge.

"Imagination is the beginning of creation. You imagine what you desire, you will what you imagine, and at last you create what you will."

George Bernard Shaw

Exponential Potential

I want you to know the reason I kept coming back to this topic: the imagination. It is because *it excites me.* I am excited about the wild diversity that lives in the realm of the imagination. I am excited by what I believe you could create out of thoughts -- out of your heartbeat -- the sheer energy of all your imaginations -- lifting up of all that potential.

A Word About Historical Precedent

We are told that it is foolish to look to the future while ignoring the past. Yet what we see when we cast our glance back is only the dismal failure of past cultures to address the future. I say, let history go. Use very little of the past in creating the future. We have reached a point of exponential expansion that we could never have measured, and history cannot repeat itself. Indeed it has not repeated itself in decades -- for the world's ever compounding population dictates new territory -- new frontiers of potential -- year by year.

We cannot apply historical models to a world with billions of inhabitants. Billions of minds. Billions of dreams. Billions of energetic desires. The vibration of billions of hearts.

This is a new phenomenon. These are new criteria and new ways of being. This is a new world of possibility. We need active imaginations and a deliberate choosing of the dream, together. We are called upon to work to the edge of our ability to secure these dreams.

And we are given what we need to make it through to the next place.

You see, through all the narrowing of attitudes and options we have perceived for many decades, that whole time, abundance has always poured forth. Its passage through our lives was restricted. The dominant energies have been so stingy, so punitive, so mean. Sisters, the dam is breaking. We must get ready for a deluge of joy, a sort of orgasm of the universe. During this time we are evolving from lack-based cultural beings. We are moving on to a center of abundance.

Use these tools to shift your seat on the mandala, thus changing the entire context. Let your imagination feed it all back to you, in your journal, in your quiet space. Take this information and imagine again, a huge, expanded vision, an absolute hallucination of a glorious future.

Writing Exercise
1) Look back over your notes you've made while reading this book. Do you see bits of your personal vision emerging? Write from those little pieces. Take a highlighter to your journal, and mark words and passages that touch you. Make a list from these for future deepening of your journey. These are real clues from your imagination.

2) What are your cultural images of paradise? They probably come from your childhood, perhaps messages from the religion you were raised with. What deep assumptions have we made that tell us this can never be? Write for 20 minutes from this concept. Use it for your anthology work. Feel your deep self when you allow a utopian vision to form. The information in those feelings will tell you what to do next.

Little Shift

Breathe, smile, and relax. When you close this book, sit for a moment with it in your hands. Close your eyes and allow images to surface. You are opening to your journey, right now.

Keep letting your vision emerge. Keep expanding the limits, adding elements from the dreams of others whom you admire. And please, relax. Take any or all of these suggestions and turn them into a part of your life. Look at your notes. Search them for clues your imagination is sending through, clues to your best next step. Keep writing. Exhale fully. And reach out to your community. You are here for a reason. There is a portal hidden in your life -- there may be many. Every day gives an opportunity to enter. Prepare to transform.

What deepens you deepens all:
We all need what you need.

I DOUBLE DARE YOU

If you have not done a single exercise in this book, I double dare you to do this -- just this one. Take this moment to sit quietly with your feet on the floor, and summon your imagination. See yourself sitting in an empty room. From some corner a voice speaks to you. Over and over, you hear the same words: "all is forgiven." Allow yourself to hear this message, over, and over, and over. When you finish reading this, put the book down and walk to the kitchen. Pour yourself a glass of water and drink it. Continue the words in your mind, like a gentle counting. All is forgiven, all is forgiven, all is forgiven. Keep hearing it until you feel a physical shift. Hold a glass of water in your hand and look at it as you repeat these words. Remember this whenever you fill a glass for yourself or your beloveds. Allow it to go on in the background, for hours, for days, forever. More than anything else in this book, this one shift will release energy and open you to the ecstatic power of your imagination.

I call this a pure liquid blessing. If you can give yourself this one quiet exercise, if you can allow these words even as you create them, you are ready for Eden.

REFERENCES, RESOURCES, and BOOKS I RECOMMEND

The resources listed here are meant as a jumping-off point. For those of you who need guidance as you learn to do research online, go ahead and start with these websites. Most websites include a "links" section. Links give you another way into all that the World Wide Web has to offer. I often start a search by going to a trusted website, hitting some of their links, and continuing from there.

Suzanna's website:
www.crowsmoons.com

This is the website for my publishing company, Crow's Moons Productions. Here you will find the links to my other projects, workshops and books. I am looking to my readers for information about your lives, your needs, your concerns. Please come visit!

WRITING AND SELF PUBLISHING

www.bookcoaching.com, Judy Cullins
She has a down to earth approach for helping writers reach their goals. Read her many free articles and subscribe to her e-zine.

www.parapublishing.com, Dan Poynter
His e-zine always has several items of current relevance to the writing and publishing world

www.writesoftheimagination.com
Check out their online classes

www.newsociety. com
A Canadian publisher with integrity. Read their criteria regarding publishing.

WOMEN'S WEBSITES

womensenews.org
Women's E-News
Geared toward news of women's issues.

www.phenomenalwomen.com
Phenomenal Women: Website for women with websites! Great place to go see what women are doing on the Internet. You could spend a lot of time just looking at all the women's websites included here.

www.seedfusion.com: Lynne Franks. The SEED Network is a global community of entrepreneurial women of spirit dedicated to personal empowerment and positive social change.

www.joannamacy.net
Joanna Macy is one of our precious planetary resources. She clearly and compassionately articulates the current needs of the planet while offering several paths of action. Be sure to read "Joanna's Letters" and "The Great Turning."

GOOD NEWS, INSPIRATION and COMFORT

www.zeri.org
(zero emissions research and initiatives)
This institute is designed to develop and implement environmentally sustainable solutions to humanity's needs. If you don't know about ZERI, you must visit their website. Look at the theory page and the FAQs. Their work is the type of core work we need in order to coalesce our diversity and visions into one focused outcome. They have attracted many effective industries and receive support from the United Nations.

www.yesmagazine.com
YES!Magazine is devoted to spreading the word about the powerful positive forces at work on our future culture. Available in paper version also.

www.culturalcreatives.org
Paul Ray's website continues the discussion and dissemination of information concerning the group he and Sherry Anderson named "Cultural Creatives," the 50-million-plus-in-the-U.S.-alone group that "remains invisible to mainstream press" but may very well be responsible for altering history rapidly and profoundly.

RESOURCES FOR SUSTAINABILITY

www.lead.org
LEAD International
Calculate your ecological footprint. This is an excellent first step to discovering how much of the earth's resources you are using in an average year. The web page for this calculation is: http://www.lead.org/leadnet/footprint/

www.globalideasbank.org
The Global Ideas Bank
This is an amazing website and an amazing organization. Take a look at all the social invention going on all around the world, and presented in an accessible form on this website. This site has so many links and exciting places to go, set aside a chunk of time so you can really get a good look at it.

www.bioneers.org
BIONEERS
A site full of visionaries and the work of restoration of this planet. Sections include Green Media; Natural Design; Natural Medicine; Activism; Environmental Education; Organic Food, Farming, & Seeds; Nature, Culture & Spirit; Green Entrepreneurship; Cultural & Biological Diversity; and the indigenous perspective, Through Indigenous Eyes.

www.commondreams.org
Common Dreams
For alternative news and many alternative writers.

www.earthcharter. org
The Earth Charter Initiative
View the Earth Charter, learn how it came about, and see other activities geared toward peace.

www.organicconsumers.org
Organic Consumers
Understand what is happening with large-scale food production, including genetic modification and other issues.

www.fungi.com
Fungi Perfecti
Mushrooms can save the world. If you don't believe it, go to this website and click on "mycotechnology." Read Paul Stamets' explanation of mycoremediation.

www.bfi.org
The Buckminster Fuller Institute.
Bucky Fuller's inspired vision of a sustainable world continues to play a major role in the development of solutions.

www.sustainablebusiness.com
Sustainable Business
Full-service website with news items, directories, green investment information. Excellent alternative media.

www.secondnature.org
Education for sustainability. Works with colleges and universities. Outreach and advocacy.

Websites change and rearrange all the time. Please check in with me on my website at www.crowsmoons.com for a continuing list of new excitement online. I want to hear from you when you come across a new online business so I can include it on my website! Keep in touch, my friends.

BOOKS LIST

Building Your Skills as a Visionary Citizen

Making The Gods Work For You. Caroline W. Casey, Harmony, 1998.
"...an effective, imaginative language through which we can unravel the mystery and beauty of the gifts we have brought for each other and discover the joy of offering those gifts fully."

The Hebrew Alphabet, A Mystical Journey. Edward Hoffman, Chronicle Books, 1998.
"A guide to inner development through the study and meditation of Hebrew letters."

Skillful Means. Tarthang Tulku, Dharma Publishing, 1991
From the back cover: Here is a book about LOVING WORK. About making human values -- integrity, responsibility, creativity, caring -- the heart of all activity. This book shows how to make your work an expression of your total being, a means to create harmony and balance in yourself and in the world.

<u>Think On Your Feet, The Art of Thinking and Speaking Under Pressure</u>. Kenneth Wydro, Spectrum, 1981.
"...Shows how to tap the hidden potential of the imagination. Develops the ability to move, think, speak and create spontaneously... how to use relaxation, trust, concentration and sensory awareness exercises to develop self-confidence."

Progressive & Alternative Health Ideas

<u>Tony&Tina Color Energy</u>. Cristina Bornstein & Anthony Gill, Simon and Schuster, 2002
How Color Can Transform Your Life. "... shows us how to consciously use the power of color as a healing tool in our daily lives."

<u>Brain Longevity</u>. Dr. Khalsa, Warner, 1997.
"I believe Alzheimer's disease can be delayed and prevented. I believe that age-associated memory impairment can be eradicated. I believe that people in the forties, fifties, sixties and beyond can not only retain an almost perfect memory but also have "youthful minds" -- minds characterized by the dynamic brain power, learning ability, creativity and emotional zest generally found only in young people. I'm positive because of one central reason: the clinical results I have achieved."

Making Businesses In The New World

Quantum Creativity, Nine Principles to Transform the Way You Work. Pamela Meyer, Contemporary Books, 2000.
"With nine simple principles and the wisdom of quantum physics, improvisation, and new management models, you can release creative passion in your workplace that will help you energize and innovate in every aspect of your job."

The Self-Publishing Manual. Dan Poynter, Para Publishing, 2000.
"This manual is your complete reference for writing, printing, publishing, promoting, marketing and distributing books."

The Soul of a Business. Tom Chappell, Bantam Books, 1993.
"A fascinating journey by a new breed of entrepreneur who is rewriting the rules of the marketplace around a profound premise: The firms that prosper will be the ones that successfully blend traditional business know-how with doing good -- for people and for the environment."

The Seed Handbook, The Feminine Way to Create Business. Lynne Franks, Tarcher/Putnam, 2000.
"The SEED Handbook (Sustainable Enterprise and Empowerment Dynamics) is a ten-stage program that is both an economic and a personal growth tool. Offering practical as well as meditative exercises, it gives you the confidence to trust your abilities, passions, and values to enable yourself to create something organic that grows naturally from who you are as a person."

Visions Of The Future

The Fabric of The Future, Women Visionaries Illuminate the Path to Tomorrow. Edited by M.J.Ryan, Conari Press, 1998.
"...you will not find wildly fantastic predictions on the life-changing nature of technology, the design of work spaces in outer space, or the sexual practices of mutant humans. Rather, with their listening eyes and vision-seeking hearts, these writers invite all of us to pursue a passionate optimism in a future grounded in the emerging, evolving, and enduring values of women's spirituality."

The Cultural Creatives, How 50 Million People Are Changing The World. Paul H. Ray, Ph.D., and Sherry Ruth Anderson, Ph.D., Harmony Books, 2000.
"...They have put their finger on the pulse of an entire generation... spectacular, inspiring good news: our long-desired sea change has occurred, each of us 'cultural creatives' is not alone, together we now amount to a critical mass sufficient to transform America... 50 million pioneers who have broken out of the cultural trance and are creating effective change in the world."

FASTER, The Acceleration of Just About Everything. James Gleick, Vintage Books, 2000
"...the most advanced cases of "hurry sickness" punch 88 seconds on the microwave instead of 90 because it's faster to tap the same digit twice. Yet ... there still seems to be less time to spare."

Cradle To Cradle, Remaking the Way We Make Things. William McDonough & Michael Braungart, North Point Press, 2002.
"... Why not challenge the belief that human industry must damage the natural world? In fact, why not take nature itself as our model for making things?

NOTES

NOTES

NOTES

NOTES

NOTES

NOTES

ABOUT THE AUTHOR

Suzanna Stinnett was born in 1955 in Lawton, Oklahoma. It is her belief that humanity is poised to spontaneously redesign our global destiny into one of sustainable abundance and fulfillment for all. Toward that end, she is devoted to expanding optimism and nurturing the individual vision through her books and workshops. More of her writing can be seen at www.crowsmoons.com. She currently resides in Sebastopol, California with her husband Patrick and their dog Daisy.

ISBN 1553953266